I0824142

Breaking Through

Breaking Through

HOW ORDINARY BELIEVERS EXPERIENCE EXTRAORDINARY FREEDOM

Allen Parr
Creator of THE BEAT

An Imprint of Thomas Nelson

Breaking Through

Published by Nelson Books, an imprint of Thomas Nelson, 501 Nelson Place, Nashville, TN 37214, USA. Nelson Books and Thomas Nelson are registered trademarks of HarperCollins Christian Publishing, Inc.

Thomas Nelson titles may be purchased in bulk for educational, business, fundraising, or sales promotional use. For information, please email SpecialMarkets@ThomasNelson.com.

ISBN 978-1-4002-3981-8 (ePub)
ISBN 978-1-4002-3979-5 (HC)

HarperCollins Publishers, Macken House, 39/40 Mayor Street Upper, Dublin 1, D01 C9W8, Ireland (https://www.harpercollins.com)

Library of Congress Control Number: 2026934372

Art direction: Curt Diepenhorst
Cover design: Jay Smith
Interior design: Kristina Juodenas

Printed in the United States of America

26 27 28 29 30 LBC 5 4 3 2 1

To my wife, Jennifer, the love of my life and my #1 fan

CONTENTS

PREFACE

In 2010 I hit rock bottom. At that time, I was a single minister and seminary graduate who had been celibate for nearly fifteen years. Though many things about my life were wonderful, I found myself frustrated, angry, and extremely disappointed in God. "Why am I not married yet? What's wrong with me? Why can't I make a relationship work? Why are all my other friends married and having children, and I'm still single?" Instead of seeing my singleness as a gift, I saw it as a curse. These thoughts, and many others, were dominating my mind as I tried to make sense of my singleness.

While singleness is a noble Christian calling, and by no means a "second-class" status, I felt *called* to marriage. I wanted it. So to ensure I wasn't missing something important, I decided to seek professional counseling to gain insight into what might be under the surface for me. Through that counseling, I began to understand that because of repeated exposure to divorce within my family of origin, I was wrestling with a fear of commitment. "What if I get married and it ends up in divorce like my other family members' marriages? Or what if I get married and quickly realize I married the wrong person? Then I'll be stuck and miserable forever!" These fears dominated my thinking—but *quietly*. As a result of their secret influence, I found myself looking for a perfect girl, thinking that if I could find my ideal woman, her perfection would safeguard me from experiencing the pain of divorce. As a result, for fifteen years I was on a relational hamster wheel. I moved in and out of relationships, all of which led to heartache, pain, and disappointment. At times it felt like my quest for love was a revolving door, which a new woman would enter every few months, only to turn right back around.

Another question that filled my mind during this time was, "What in the world do I do with my sexual desires?" The way I saw it, I had three choices: I could get married, but because of my family-of-origin issues, marriage was a barrier for me and something I knew should not be forced or rushed into. My second option was to "sleep around." I mean, appealing, right? And really, who had to know?

But then I began to weigh the cost. I could get a casual partner pregnant. I could contract a sexually transmitted disease. If it became publicly known that I was sleeping around, my reputation as a minister would be tarnished, and opportunities to serve, along with my paid position at the church, would be compromised. It could ruin my life. Ruin other lives too. I could hurt another sister in Christ by misleading her into thinking I was serious about her, only for her to quickly realize I was only interested in using her body. And most importantly, I knew God would not be pleased with this behavior. So, yeah, this option was out for me.

This left me only one option: self-pleasure. This seemed to be the only safe option for me, and I found ways to justify it—again and again. "It's not hurting anyone else," I thought. "God will understand because doing this is more honorable than fornicating."

I even blamed God: "If God didn't want me to do this, He would have sent me my wife by now. So it's His fault!" And finally, "I'm not watching pornography while doing it, so it's okay." It's a bit embarrassing to admit it in as public a setting as a book, but a habit that began in my early teens turned into an all-out addiction. The worst part about it all was that no one else really knew. It became my "secret sin." I led worship every Sunday. I taught Bible study every Wednesday night. As a seminary graduate, I knew that the Bible said Jesus died to set me free, but my reality didn't line up with my theology, and I found myself in bondage to something that I did not want in my life.

I read Scripture and listened to countless sermons about how Jesus could set me free. I even preached sermons and taught others about the power of God to set *them* free, but I failed to experience that freedom in my own life. I knew it theologically but was still left questioning, "But why don't I feel free? Why do I feel so bound?"

Maybe you're at a place where I was in 2010, and you wonder if *true* freedom is even possible. Perhaps you've tried everything, whether it's prayer, accountability, church, or something else, but that one issue just keeps resurfacing in your life. You've confessed and repented, but it still feels like a huge chain around your soul. And you've silently questioned whether absolute freedom is possible. Maybe it's an emotional weight like anxiety or depression, and you've convinced yourself that freedom, joy, and peace are unattainable.

I'm here to encourage you: Freedom is possible. But it may not come the way you expect it to come.

You're in a spiritual battle, and you can't fight spiritual battles with surface-level solutions. That's what this book is all about: recognizing the chains that have quietly held you back for far too long, and walking through a biblical, practical process to break through *finally*.

Throughout this book, I'll refer to these internal bondages as *soul chains*. Like physical chains, they bind you. But instead of your body, they bind your soul—your mind, will, and emotions. But the good news is that Jesus came to break every soul chain, no matter how long you've carried it. I define a soul chain as "a deeply entrenched mindset, habit, or spiritual barrier that opposes God's truth and keeps a person in bondage, shaping their thoughts, behaviors, and identity in a way that hinders true freedom in Christ."

In the first chapter, we will break this definition down phrase by phrase. However, before we proceed, I want you to know for sure that Jesus can break any soul chain you may be dealing with. In Matthew

12:22–37, there is a story of a demon-possessed man who was blind and couldn't speak. He was brought to Jesus. Jesus healed the man, enabling him to both see and speak.

Many in the crowd were amazed at His miraculous power! But of course, the Pharisees began to question and accuse, saying, "No wonder he can cast out demons. He gets his power from Satan, the prince of demons" (verse 24 NLT). Jesus then began to explain how absurd it would be for Satan to cast out his own demons. If Satan empowered Jesus, why would Jesus cast a demon of Satan out of a man? It didn't make sense.

Then Jesus made this startling statement: "For who is powerful enough to enter the house of a strong man and plunder his goods? Only someone even stronger—someone who could tie him up and then plunder his house" (verse 29 NLT). It's critical to understand the imagery here. The strong man in this story is Satan (or any oppressive force). The house is a person's life. The goods are the evil areas of bondage (soul chains) established within that house (lust, fear, anger, habits, anxiety, addictions). The one who ties up the strong man is Jesus, making Him the Stronger Man. Plundering represents Jesus reclaiming what the strong man stole (freedom, identity, truth). While Christians cannot be demon-possessed like non-Christians can, the Enemy often erects these soul chains within our minds, chaining us to lies, fear, shame, or sin. This story illustrates a powerful truth: If Satan is the strong man, Jesus is the Stronger Man who can destroy every soul chain and reclaim what rightfully belongs to Him—your soul.

I am writing this book as an encouragement to anyone who has or is experiencing a soul chain in their life (and there are many different kinds that we will explore in this book). I have wrestled with and broken through many soul chains in my life. I'll be sharing them with you throughout this book. Because I'm on the other side of many of them, I'm confident you can break through as well.

As we will explore later, this does not mean I'm claiming a life of perfection. But it does mean that I am walking in the freedom that Christ died for. I am walking in purity, no longer bound by a soul chain of lust. I have a great marriage and a beautiful family, no longer living with a perpetual fear of divorce.

I want you to know that no matter what it looks like right now, soul chains can be broken in Jesus's name. I am not a professional counselor, and this book should not be used as a substitute for professional counseling. I have personally benefited greatly from counseling, including both individual and marriage counseling. With that said, I do believe the promise in God's Word in 2 Peter 1:3, which says, "By his divine power, God has given us everything we need for living a godly life. We have received all of this by coming to know him, the one who called us to himself by means of his marvelous glory and excellence" (NLT). God has provided what we need to experience true freedom, and this book will guide you biblically on how to experience that.

Why This Book Matters to You

You may find yourself struggling with these unseen battles, soul chains designed to keep you trapped in fear, addiction, negative thought patterns, or habitual sins. These struggles are so deeply rooted that they don't just affect your spiritual walk with God; they can influence your relationships, mental and emotional well-being, and even your overall sense of purpose. The challenge is that these demonic soul chains are not always obvious. Some are disguised as personality traits, past wounds, or habits you've just learned to live with, making them even harder to identify and overcome.

You may desperately want to change but feel powerless to do so. You find yourself cycling through temporary fixes that never lead to lasting transformation. This book is written to help you recognize these soul chains and, more importantly, break free from them once and for all. Through biblical teaching, practical application, and real-life testimonies, this book will guide you on your own personal journey from bondage to freedom as we break the soul chains and step into a life of true spiritual freedom.

In addition, there is an alarming rise in misinformation about deliverance, spiritual warfare, and what freedom in Christ really looks like. Many Christians believe that true freedom requires some esoteric, mystical experience at a deliverance crusade. Or sadly, some Christians may even be convinced that they are demon-possessed.

The Enemy is actively deceiving, distracting, and discouraging believers, keeping them bound in lies that limit their ability to express and live out their faith and walk in their divine purpose and calling. Soul chains don't just affect the person; they can and always do impact marriages, families, churches, and entire communities. In other words, the stakes are high, which is why I am writing this book. I want to help you recognize the lies that have kept you bound, rediscover your true identity in Christ, and begin living in the freedom Jesus has already secured for you through the cross.

What to Expect

Sadly, discussions around spiritual warfare often fall into two extremes. Either the process is overspiritualized, making it feel mystical and totally out of reach, or it's reduced to mere behavior modification, treating soul chains as nothing more than bad habits that can be fixed with more willpower. Neither approach fully addresses the problem's depth or provides a lasting solution. This book takes a different approach by focusing on deeply biblical and efficient principles, thereby equipping you with a clear, actionable road map to inner healing and lasting freedom.

Instead of focusing on symptoms alone (sins, struggles, emotional pain, etc.), I tackle the root causes of soul chains: the lies we believe, the spiritual forces at work, and the negative patterns we've unknowingly accepted and reinforced over time.

This book is structured to take you on a three-part journey.

Part 1: Understanding the Problem (chapters 1–3): We must begin by understanding the *problem* we face as believers. Here I aim to provide an understanding of precisely what soul chains are, the different types, how they form, how to recognize them, and the impact they have on our lives. It may feel a bit bumpy at times, but this is the essential work required to experience true freedom and healing.

Part 2: Walking Through the Process (chapters 4–7): Once we expose the problem, we will provide a clear, step-by-step biblical strategy, or *process*, for dismantling soul chains, renewing the mind, and experiencing long-lasting freedom (something we all desire).

Part 3: Embracing the Promise (chapters 8–10): Finally, I want you to start envisioning what true freedom can look like in your life and to understand that it's not only possible but also already promised and available through Christ.

In this book I seek to strike a healthy balance between external influences (such as generational cycles or demonic oppression) and personal responsibility. While I acknowledge the presence of spiritual realities, I also want to empower believers to take action. In other words, God will do His part, but we must also do ours. This book will not promise an instant breakthrough, but it will equip you with the tools you need to obtain and sustain genuine, lifelong transformation.

I'm inviting you to not just read this book but go on a transformational journey with me. I pray you're encouraged by the many stories I share from my own life as well as from the lives of others who have broken through. Take time to reflect on your own life and complete the reflection questions at the end of each chapter. My ultimate goal is that by the end of this journey, you won't just understand freedom; you'll be walking in it.

One of the biggest lies the Enemy wants you to believe is that you can't change. He wants you to think that where you are now is where you'll always be. Trust me, I know, because I believed that lie for years. He wants you to feel you're the only one experiencing a soul chain. He wants you to think that if your family struggles with certain things, you will likely experience the same struggles. He wants you to be convinced that you'll always be bound by your struggles and past mistakes, or that the sins you've committed are too deeply rooted to overcome. The reality is that he wants your soul chains to become your identity. The good news I want you to embrace from this book is this: Jesus didn't just die to save us from sin—He saved us for freedom (John 8:36).

Did you catch that? Jesus didn't just die for you to go to heaven. He died so you can experience abundant life (total freedom in Christ) right now on earth. Freedom is not just reserved for the spiritually elite Christians; it's for you! I want you to imagine, not a perfect life, but a life characterized by righteousness, peace, joy, clarity, purity, and purpose. As you read, you'll find that some chapters may be more challenging than others. You may feel resistance internally and even spiritually. Why? Because the Enemy doesn't want you to be free. However, I want to encourage you to face the challenge, knowing that a beautiful life of freedom awaits you on the other side.

So I invite you to embrace the journey! Answer the reflection questions. Take your time. Read this book while journaling your thoughts to help you embrace the principles and experience true transformation. Commit to this process and let the Holy Spirit transform you from the inside out as we walk together. Ask God to truly reveal what He wants to heal, break, and restore in your life. And I pray that you won't have just read about freedom by the end of this journey; you'll be living it. This is your official invitation to transformation.

PART 1

UNDERSTANDING THE PROBLEM

CHAPTER 1

TRAPPED . . . BUT DON'T KNOW IT

Several years ago a woman named Linda contacted our ministry with what seemed like a simple technical support issue: She was unable to access one of the courses she had enrolled in. I began to troubleshoot her issue, but before the conversation ended, she paused and asked, "Brother Allen, do you know how I discovered your ministry?"

I didn't. But her answer sent shock waves through my soul.

Linda had a daughter named Samantha, whom she described as bright, kind, successful, and full of promise. She was the type of daughter every parent dreams of having. But Samantha had wrestled with an internal darkness that no one in the family understood. And tragically, at just twenty-eight years old, she took her own life.

Linda's entire world shattered in that instant. As a mother, she was haunted by what-ifs: What if I had seen the signs? What if I had done more? Said more? Prayed more? Paid more attention? Called her more frequently? Asked the right questions?

That unbearable grief quickly gave way to something even more toxic—shame. Internally, Linda believed that she had failed her daughter and that her daughter's suicide was her fault. That she wasn't just grieving a loss, but living with an eternal stain on her soul.

And then came the message that broke her spirit.

Leaders at her church, whom she had trusted during this fragile time, told her that suicide was the only sin her daughter could never be forgiven for because Samantha never had the chance to repent for it. They said Samantha had gone to hell, and that Linda would never see her again. It was like a second death. She knew that the Bible described hell as a place of torment and suffering. Imagining her daughter in that vile place sent Linda to experience her own internal hell on earth.

Suddenly the God she had once trusted felt cold, distant, even cruel. She couldn't grasp how a loving God would let her daughter suffer so silently while alive and then punish her by sending her to suffer in hell upon her death. She couldn't reconcile how a church could speak such devastating words to someone already drowning in their own sorrow. Her grief quickly morphed into bitterness toward God. Shame evolved into rage, even anger toward the church. And the once-vibrant faith that had carried her through difficult times in the past was buried beneath a pile of unanswered questions and silent bitterness.

Linda began to drift spiritually. For years. Until one night in her desperation, she went to Google and typed in a simple question: Is suicide the unforgivable sin?

Providentially, she stumbled upon one of our videos. As she listened to the truth, it was like a wave of grace washed over her. She understood that suicide was simply self-murder and that God forgave people in the Bible who had murdered, like King David. If God can forgive murder, God had forgiven Samantha. Linda was encouraged to know that Samantha's faith in Jesus was sufficient to secure eternal life. She heard, perhaps for the first time in years, that suicide is not the unforgivable sin. That God's grace reaches further than our darkest moments. That salvation is based on Christ's finished work—not the way our story ends.

She wept. Not simply because the video had given her an answer but because it gave her hope. For the first time in years, Linda felt the chains loosen. The shame began to lift. The bitterness started to melt. And in her place of despair, the truth began to bloom: God had not forsaken her, and He had not forsaken Samantha either.

Linda's story shows us something powerful: Soul chains are not always loud and obvious. Sometimes they form in the quiet corners of grief, unanswered prayers, or, quite frankly, bad theology. But just as those chains form, they can be broken. God's truth has the power to meet us in our personal pits, rewrite our pain, and gently lead us back to hope.

Let's return to the working definition we introduced in the introduction: "A soul chain is a deeply entrenched mindset, habit, or spiritual barrier that opposes God's truth and keeps a person in bondage, shaping their thoughts, behaviors, and identity in a way that hinders true freedom in Christ."

Soul Chains Defined

Let's take some time to break this definition down so that you fully understand what a soul chain is before we discuss how they are formed in our lives.

"deeply entrenched"

Notice that a soul chain is a "deeply entrenched mindset, habit, or spiritual barrier." The word "entrenched" means deeply rooted and difficult to remove. Soul chains live beneath the surface. Notice this. Inherent in the term *soul chain* is something that makes you feel "chained" or trapped.

These aren't just everyday struggles but rather established patterns of thinking or behavior that become so ingrained that they feel natural to a person, even though they contradict God's truth. They can be thoughts like

- I'll never be truly happy.
- I don't have a true purpose to live for.
- I'll never be able to overcome this addiction.
- I'll never experience true love again.
- God can never forgive me for what I've done.

"that opposes God's truth"

The key component of soul chains is that they oppose what God says is true. They are built on deception. They twist what God says, replacing His truth with distorted perspectives that feel true but are actually lies.

A similar term frequently used to describe this experience is *stronghold*. Soul chains and strongholds are very closely related. Paul described strongholds as "arguments and every pretension that *sets itself up against the knowledge of God*" (2 Corinthians 10:5).

"and keeps a person in bondage"

A soul chain is much stronger than just a wrong belief; it is a prison. It keeps a person trapped in unhealthy cycles, often without the believer being fully aware of the damage it's causing. These cycles could include being stuck in unhealthy relationships, addiction, overcommitting due to the soul chain of people-pleasing, constantly comparing yourself to others on social media, or lashing out at loved ones because of repressed anger.

Many people trapped in soul chains genuinely desire change, but the deeply ingrained nature of these false beliefs makes freedom seem impossible. Jesus came to set the captives free (Luke 4:18), but soul chains make it hard for people to receive that freedom because they have been conditioned to believe that their situation, sin, or struggle is permanent. Without realizing it, they begin to accept the chains as part of their identity, rather than recognizing them as something that can be broken.

"shaping their thoughts, behaviors, and identity"

Soul chains do more than just influence a person's thinking; they shape their entire outlook on life. Over time, these false beliefs become so ingrained that they feel like absolute truth, making it difficult to recognize them as lies. A person who has lived under the weight of a soul chain for years may not even question it, as it has become an integral part of their mental and emotional framework. It affects how a person responds to life's challenges, whether with faith or fear, confidence or insecurity. It also dictates how a person relates to God, whether they see Him as a loving Father or a harsh taskmaster. Instead of seeing themselves as children of God who can walk in freedom, they begin to accept bondage as part of who they are.

The good news is that our soul chains do not determine our identity; God's truth does. However, as long as these deceptive mindsets remain unchallenged, they will continue negatively affecting the believer. We will discuss the greater impact of these soul chains in a later chapter.

"hindering true freedom in Christ"

This is the most significant consequence of being tied to a soul chain. It hinders a person's ability to experience freedom and live the abundant life Jesus offers by way of His sacrifice on the cross. It's not that freedom isn't available; it's that the soul chain is so deeply entrenched that it blinds the minds and hearts of people, leaving them convinced that freedom is impossible.

All right, so now that we're clear on what a soul chain is, it's time to move on and discuss how these demonic chains form in our lives. I propose that they are formed in four primary ways: lies, sin patterns, emotional wounds, and cultural influences. Let's break them all down.

Soul Chains Are Formed Through Lies

Every soul chain begins with a lie. Whether it's a lie about God, ourselves, sin, or the world, deception is the foundation that allows the Enemy to gain real estate in our souls and minds. If Satan can get us to believe something false as if it were true, that belief will begin to dominate our lives. This is why Jesus said, "You will know the truth, and the truth will set you free" (John 8:32), because freedom comes when we replace deception with truth (more on this later).

For example, if someone believes the lie that they will never be good enough, this can ultimately lead to a soul chain of perfectionism, anxiety, people-pleasing, or self-hatred. Or if they believe the lie that "God is angry with me and can't really love me after what I've done," then this will undoubtedly lead to a soul chain of legalism, where they feel as though they must earn God's love by living a perfect life. Or let's say a young lady grew up hearing or feeling that she is worthless. This may form into a soul chain of insecurity, leading to unhealthy relationships, fear of rejection, and a series of poor relational decisions.

Soul Chains Are Formed Through Sin Patterns

One of the most common ways in which soul chains are formed is not through lies but through repeated sinful behaviors. Because these are so common, I warn you that things may get a little bumpy before they get better. When sin becomes a habit, it reinforces a thinking pattern, making it feel normal, inevitable, necessary, and unchangeable. Over time, what starts as a single compromise turns into a deeply ingrained cycle, creating a soul chain of bondage that seems impossible to break.

The Enemy uses sin cycles to keep believers trapped, feeding them the lie that they are powerless to change. But the truth is, sin does not have to define us, and soul chains do not have to control us.

Romans 6:14 says, "Sin shall no longer be your master, because you are not under the law, but under grace." Well, thanks, Paul. You make it sound so easy! Before we can break through, we need to understand how sin patterns form into soul chains and why they are so perilous. It's essential to recognize that sin is not merely an isolated action; it is a complex process. This is precisely how a soul chain of sin is formed.

A key scripture that outlines this process is James 1:14–15: "Each person is tempted when they are dragged away by their own evil desire and enticed. Then, after desire has conceived, it gives birth to sin; and sin, when it is full-grown, gives birth to death."

Notice the progression here. It begins with our sinful *desires*. We all have fleshly desires that conflict with our spiritual desires. Next, we are *enticed*. The imagery here is like bait in the water seeking to ensnare a fish. This is the heart of the *temptation*. Then, when our *desires* are unchecked, they give birth to action, which leads to *sin*. Because the very nature of sin is progressive, when it matures, it becomes *full-grown*. At this point, our sin leads to *death*. This could be the death of our intimacy with God, our peace and joy, a relationship, or possibly eternal death for non-Christians who don't turn to God.

To make this process easier to understand, here are five steps that explain how sin becomes a soul chain. My ultimate goal is that you'll self-identify what step you may be in, so that a habitual sin soul chain doesn't develop in your life.

Step 1: The open door to bondage

Sadly, a single act of disobedience can open the door to sin, activate our fleshly desires, and create a craving to engage again. At first, it may seem harmless, minor, or insignificant, but it opens the door for deeper spiritual entanglement. This is Satan's plan. Satan loves to get us to focus on the *short-term pleasures* while hiding the *long-term consequences* of sin.

Satan rarely tempts believers with full-blown bondage up front; he entices them to take just one step in the wrong direction, knowing that if they get a taste of the temporary pleasures of sin and compromise once, it will be easier to compromise again.

Sin is like a seed. Once it's been planted, it begins to grow roots. We may feel guilty the first time we compromise, but we convince ourselves that we can manage it, so it's not a big deal. The Enemy uses this moment to desensitize our conscience, making future sin easier to justify (more on this in step 3).

Not too long ago, I received an email from someone who reached out to our ministry for help. For privacy purposes, we will refer to him as Brett. As many men do, Brett reached out because he was struggling with a porn addiction. As he explained his struggle in the email, it followed the five steps we will outline here. Brett is forty, and when he was thirteen, he stumbled upon some magazines his father had hidden in the basement. He opened a *Playboy* magazine and was immediately fascinated by what he saw. His eyes had never seen a naked woman before, and from that day forward, he could not get those images out of his mind. Shortly after that, his father must have moved the magazines to another part of the house, because Brett could no longer find them. Since this was in the nineties, Brett's access to porn was restricted, but the door had been opened.

Here's the principle for step 1: Sin rarely begins in full force. It starts with one compromise that makes the next one easier. But it doesn't stop with just one sin. The Enemy's goal is to take us as far down this process as possible, which leads to step 2.

Step 2: The birth of a habit

The soul chain of sin strengthens its grip when sin moves from a one-time action to a repeated pattern. What was once a single compromise now becomes a habit, a repeated behavior that starts shaping a person's decisions, thought processes, and desires. At this stage, the person knows what they're doing is wrong, but the initial guilt they felt after the first sin begins to fade, making it easier to repeat the behavior.

What makes this stage so dangerous is that sin is seldom static. It either gets weaker through repentance or stronger through repetition. The more a person engages in the sin, the more comfortable they become with it, and the harder it becomes to stop. This is where the Enemy begins to tighten his grip, leading the person deeper into deception and making it harder to turn back. Here's the principle for step 2: The power of sin either weakens through repentance or strengthens through repetition.

Brett continued telling us his story in his email. As access to high-speed internet became more widely available in the 2000s, the three barriers that had previously hindered him were all torn down. Porn was now *accessible* (no longer limited to magazines). It was *affordable* (no longer something you had to pay for). And it was *anonymous* (no one needed to know). He began bingeing inappropriate content for hours at a time. The habit had formed.

Step 3: The shift in thinking

Soul chains become even more fortified when a person begins to justify the sin in their mind. This is very common because the Holy Spirit convicts believers of sin, which is uncomfortable. So they naturally try to find ways to relieve this spiritual discomfort, and justifying the sin is the easiest and most common way.

What was once a clear moral boundary now seems flexible, and the person convinces themself that their sin is excusable, necessary, or even acceptable. This is where the conscience erodes and the soul chain becomes even more fortified.

This process is known as *justification*, the mental and emotional reasoning we use to make sin seem less, well, sinful. It happens when we stop feeling conviction and instead begin to rationalize and defend our behavior. Paul described this process vividly in Ephesians 4:18–19, "They are darkened in their understanding and separated from the life of God because of the ignorance that is in them due to the hardening of their hearts. Having lost all sensitivity, they have given themselves over to sensuality so as to indulge in every kind of impurity, and they are full of greed."

Notice Paul said here that they "lost all sensitivity," resulting in them giving "themselves over to sensuality so as to indulge in every kind of impurity." Ouch! Thanks a lot, Paul.

See, at this stage, the heart becomes calloused, and the sin that once felt wrong now feels normal. The longer the justification continues, the more dangerous the soul chain becomes. The Bible warns that our consciences can be seared, meaning that if we justify sin long enough, we will no longer feel the same level of guilt or conviction that once held us back.

Once again, Paul said in 1 Timothy 4:1–2, "The Spirit clearly says that in later times some will abandon the faith and follow deceiving spirits and things taught by demons. Such teachings come through hypocritical liars, whose consciences have been seared as with a hot iron."

The phrase "seared as with a hot iron" refers to how scar tissue loses sensitivity after being burned. The same thing happens spiritually; when we ignore conviction, we lose the ability to feel it.

- The first time we sin? We feel guilt and conviction.
- The second time? The guilt lessens.
- The third, fourth, and fifth times? We start justifying it.
- Eventually it doesn't feel wrong anymore.

This is precisely what happened with Brett. Brett got married and assumed that marriage would cure his problem. But to his disappointment, the habit only intensified. Because his mind had been conditioned to be aroused only at novelty, he noticed that his desire for his wife began to diminish. This left his sexual needs unmet, and he turned even more frequently to porn. Only this time, he justified it. He thought, "Well, at least I'm not cheating on my wife." And, "If my wife were meeting my needs the way I want her to, I wouldn't have to resort to this."

That may be Brett's story, but here are some common ways in which we all justify our sin.

First, we justify by *minimizing sin*:

- It's not that big of a deal.
- Everyone struggles with something.
- At least I'm not doing something worse.

Second, we justify sin by *comparing ourselves to others*:

- I know other people who do way worse things than I do.
- I know Christians who do this and still serve God in ministry, so God must not be too angry with them.

Third, we justify sin by *blaming our circumstances*:

- If I were married, I wouldn't have to commit this sin.
- I'm just doing what I must do right now to survive.
- If my spouse were to meet my needs, then I wouldn't have to look at porn.

Fourth, we justify sin by making *spiritual excuses*:

- God understands my heart.
- If it were really that bad, God would have stopped me.
- If God didn't want me to struggle with this, He would have changed my situation by now so that I didn't have to continue doing this.

- I'll stop when the time is right. God knows I'm working on this.
- If God didn't want me to act on my same-sex desires, He would not have created me this way.

Fifth, we may even justify sin by *redefining sin as something good*:

- This isn't really wrong; society just says it is. (This is particularly common with Christians who may struggle with same-sex attraction.)
- God wouldn't want me to be unhappy, so I think this is okay.
- I'm not hurting anyone, so what's the problem?

Sixth, we justify sin by *abusing grace*:

- God will forgive me anyway. He has to because I can't lose my salvation.
- We're under grace, not the law.
- God loves me no matter what, so it doesn't really matter what I do.

I know that was extremely bumpy, but it was necessary because God wants you to be free, and so do I. One step toward experiencing that freedom is recognizing and identifying the faulty thought patterns that keep you bound. Here's the principle for step 3: Every time we rationalize sin, we reinforce its grip and weaken our sensitivity to God's voice.

Step 4: The sin's comfort and control

At this stage, the person is no longer justifying sin. They are now depending on it. What started as a choice has become a necessity.

Sin can become a coping mechanism for pain or stress. The person uses sin to numb emotional pain or to avoid dealing with real issues. Instead of turning to God for strength and comfort, they turn to their addiction, toxic behavior, or destructive habit. Over time, this becomes the default way of dealing with stress, anxiety, loneliness, or fear. It could be using alcohol, social media, or drugs to escape stress, trauma, or deep pain. Or it could be using pornography or sexual sin to numb loneliness, rejection, or low self-worth.

When we become codependent on our sin, it warps our desires, making us crave it more. The more we repeat a sin, the more our minds, bodies, and souls crave it. Sin can reprogram our appetites to make what once felt wrong feel not only right but necessary. This is how it's done: When we engage in any sort of pleasurable activity, whether it's sexual sin, eating candy, gossip, or any form of indulgence, our brain releases a chemical called dopamine. This is often referred to as "the happy hormone" because it induces a feeling of happiness, pleasure, or satisfaction. And who doesn't want more of that feeling?

God designed dopamine to reinforce good behaviors. For instance, when we fall in love, we receive regular dopamine hits that draw us back to the person we love because we repeatedly want that "feel good" feeling. However, sin hijacks this system. When we sin, dopamine is released, and the brain interprets this behavior as something rewarding, saying, "Give me more of this!" Over time, it creates a neurological craving for the same dopamine hit we had the last time. And sadly, the more we feed that desire, the more the brain builds pathways that expect and even demand that desire be met.

To make this even more straightforward to understand, let's compare it to sugar cravings. Yeah, trust me, I know . . . this is convicting! Several years ago I embarked on a life-changing health and fitness journey, losing thirty-five pounds in just over ninety days. The first thing my coach told me to do was to give up sugar. I didn't think that was possible, considering my sweet tooth. It doesn't matter if it's candy, cakes, or pies; if it's sweet, I want it! For the first few days, it was tough because my brain had been wired for so long to have sugar. It was saying, "Give it to me—now!" But when I reprogrammed it, the desire for sugar slowly faded, and the weight slowly came off. That's how sin works. Our brains need to be rewired, which we will discuss later.

Finally, it begins to feel like sin is no longer a choice. We often feel stuck and doomed to repeat the same failures over and over again. Then it can ultimately cause us to feel like we are too far gone, too weak, or too broken to change, so what's the point in trying? We might as well go ahead and yield.

Brett continued to share his story with us. After long, stressful days at work, he found himself looking forward to and making plans to consume inappropriate content online rather than spend time with his wife. He used it as a stress reliever, a sleep aid, a coping mechanism. He became dependent on it. The guilt and conviction he once experienced had long ago left him.

When sin gets to this point, it feels too deeply ingrained to break free. The person may still acknowledge that it's wrong, but now they believe they can't live without it. Their sin has become a crutch, something they repeatedly return to, even when they want to stop. They feel they are no longer in control of the sin. Instead, the sin is controlling them. Here's the principle that sums up step 4: Instead of sin being something we fall into, it becomes something we actively desire and pursue. This leads us to step 5.

Step 5: The sin as identity

At this final stage, sin is no longer just something we do; it becomes who we are. What started as a *choice* became a *habit* and eventually turned into a *dependency*, now defining our *identity*. Instead of believing that freedom is possible, the person accepts their sin as a permanent part of them. Sadly, this is very common in the LGBTQ+ community.

Many members of this community grew up in church, and they have completely identified with what many of them know deep down inside is a sin. Their sin has become their identity.

This is where the Enemy's deception reaches its fullest effect. He wants to convince a person that their struggle, addiction, or past failure is who they are at their core. At this stage, they no longer fight against the soul chain; they have come to embrace it as part of their nature.

The Bible says in Proverbs 23:7, "As he thinks in his heart, so is he" (NKJV). They fully believe the lie that they will never change (or even need to, for that matter). And that lie now shapes their identity, choices, and future.

You can tell when sin becomes a person's identity when they speak or think in ways that define them by their actions or struggles rather than by God's truth. Instead of saying, "I struggle with this," they begin to say, "This is who I am."

- I am an addict. I'll never be free from pornography.
- I was born this way. God wouldn't want me to change.
- I'm just an angry person. It's how I was raised.
- I can't let go of what they did. This is who I am now.
- I've messed up too much. God could never use someone like me.
- I'm damaged goods. No one will ever love me.

The principle is clear: Once a person identifies with their soul chain, breaking free becomes extremely difficult because they no longer see the need for freedom.

Sadly, this is what happened to Brett. He eventually got to the point where he confessed he was a porn addict. He had lost hope of ever being free. He was on the verge of losing his marriage, and he reached out to us for help.

Soul Chains Are Formed Through Emotional Wounds

Not all soul chains form through sinful patterns or repeated behaviors. Some form and take root through painful emotional experiences that leave lasting wounds. When these wounds are left unhealed, Satan exploits them, and they become an entry point for him to plant lies, distorting how a person sees themself, God, and others. Over time, these lies turn into mental and emotional soul chains, shaping their behavior and spiritual identity.

Rather than processing pain in a healthy, biblical way, people often build walls of self-protection, which can lead to bitterness, fear, distrust, and a hardened heart, which then reinforces a cycle of bondage.

The Enemy knows that a single painful event can profoundly shape a person's entire life. He uses wounds as entry points, capitalizing on moments of trauma to speak deception that a person might never have believed otherwise. For example:

- A single betrayal can create a soul chain of mistrust and isolation.
- A single rejection can plant the lie that a person is unworthy of love.
- A single traumatic experience can convince someone they will never be safe again.

Over time, these false beliefs become deeply ingrained in the heart, creating patterns of fear, bitterness, insecurity, or despair. This is why the Bible tells us in Ephesians 4:27, "Do not give the devil a foothold."

To be clear, this isn't meant to imply that *you* gave the devil a foothold, which led to the emotional wound. It simply shows that this is all that the Enemy needs to begin forming a soul chain in your life.

A foothold is an opportunity, or an entry point, where the Enemy can gain influence. Unresolved pain provides that opportunity, allowing deception to take root and grow.

Using a similar five-step process, let's dive into exactly how the Enemy exploits our open emotional wounds and forms soul chains so you can identify them in your life.

Step 1: A painful experience

Many emotional soul chains begin with a wound, a moment of deep pain, trauma, or betrayal that shakes a person's sense of security, worth, or trust. This wound can be intentional or unintentional, coming from family, friends, circumstances, or life events beyond a person's control. At this stage, the wound itself is not the soul chain, but if left unhealed, it becomes a gateway for the Enemy to plant lies that take root and reshape a person's thinking.

The Bible says in Proverbs 18:14, "The spirit of a man will sustain him in sickness, but who can bear a broken spirit?" (NKJV). This means that a broken spirit resulting from an emotional wound is harder to recover from than physical illness, because it affects one's outlook on life. We will discuss the various types of emotional wounds in the next chapter, but the pain is raw and real at this stage. The person is not yet in bondage, but they are at a crossroads. If the pain is processed with truth and healing, it can lead to growth and resilience. If left unaddressed, it can become a breeding ground for deception.

The Bible says in John 10:10, "The thief comes only to steal and kill and destroy." Satan's goal is not just to cause pain but to use that pain to steal your joy, kill your hope, and destroy your faith.

A clear picture of this is found in the story of Joseph's brothers in Genesis 37–50. We often focus a great deal on Joseph when we read his story, but seldom do we consider it from the brothers' perspective. In Genesis 37:3, we read, "Jacob loved Joseph more than any of his other children because Joseph had been born to him in his old age. So one day Jacob had a special gift made for Joseph—a beautiful robe" (NLT).

Now, imagine if this were today. Your father buys your school clothes from the thrift store (no shame in that, by the way) but gets your brother's clothes from designer boutiques. How would that make you feel? Also, imagine if you and your brother had two different mothers but lived in the same household, and it was abundantly clear that your father loved your brother more than you because he loved his mother more than he loved your mother. Can you imagine what type of emotional wound that would cause?

Perhaps you've experienced the pain of favoritism in your own home. If so, you can identify with Joseph's brothers. This open wound of rejection by their father ultimately turned into soul chains of jealousy, hatred, and even a desire for revenge. Because they didn't deal with their emotional wound of rejection, they acted out by wanting to kill Joseph and ultimately selling their own brother into slavery. The Enemy used that initial wound as an entry point for a soul chain in their lives.

Another story that vividly illustrates this is the story of Naomi in the book of Ruth. Through a series of events, Naomi lost both her husband and her two sons, leaving her widowed and childless in a foreign land (Ruth 1). Can you imagine the pain she experienced? Her grief then shaped her identity, which led her to identify herself by the name *Bitter*. In verses 19–21, we read,

> The two of them [Ruth and Naomi] continued on their journey. When they came to Bethlehem, the entire town was excited by their arrival. "Is it really Naomi?" the women asked.
>
> "Don't call me Naomi," she responded. "Instead, call me Mara, for the Almighty has made life very bitter for me. I went away full, but the LORD has brought me home empty. Why call me Naomi when the LORD has caused me to suffer and the Almighty has sent such tragedy upon me?" (NLT)

My heart breaks for her. Does yours? The Enemy exploited her open wound of loss and grief to create a soul chain of bitterness in her life.

It was 1995, and I was a junior in college attending a local church. When I began attending, I noticed that the pastor showed a special interest in me. He would often invite me and a few of my other college friends to his home. He took us out to eat. He would frequently ask me into his office to discuss things. I was also given unique opportunities to serve in ministry at the age of twenty. I sincerely thought, "Wow, a megachurch pastor wants to mentor, develop, and disciple me? This is exactly what I've been praying for." As time went on, I noticed that he would say things like, "I'm attracted to your spirit, Allen," or, "You have a beautiful spirit."

I didn't think anything of it until one day when he hugged me and proceeded to kiss me on the neck. It was then that I began putting things together. The rumors I had heard of this pastor struggling with same-sex attraction all began to make sense. Then one of my other very close friends told me the same thing had happened to him. And others began to confirm their experiences. On one hand, this was the church that was responsible for my spiritual growth. This was the church all of my friends attended. This was the church where my supposed "spiritual father" was. And yet I came to the sad conclusion that the pastor had another agenda in mind.

I share that story because maybe you've had negative experiences at churches as well. Maybe you've been disappointed because a pastor had a moral failure. Or the money was mismanaged. As a result of these negative experiences, you've become bitter toward church. I could have easily concluded, "I'll never set foot in a church again. I'll never trust a pastor again." The point is that this experience could have created a deep-seated soul chain of anger, bitterness, and distrust. But I processed it and experienced the healing that I needed, and those chains never had a chance to take root.

Consider Cameron, a forty-year-old African American man. When Cameron was ten years old, he was the only Black kid on his baseball team, but he was clearly the best. His coach was a white man. His coach would seldom allow Cameron to play in the games, unlike the other white kids. When he did, he put Cameron at the bottom of the lineup. He barely spoke to Cameron. He criticized him every time he made a mistake. On one particular occasion, after Cameron struck out, his coach said to him, "See, that's why kids like you should probably stick to basketball." Unbeknownst to him at the time, an open wound of racism was created. But the process went even deeper.

Step 2: Pain becomes deception

After experiencing significant pain, our minds immediately seek to interpret what happened and assign meaning to it. At this stage, we are vulnerable, and the Enemy loves to seize the opportunity to plant lies and deception.

Remember when I quoted John 8:32, which says, "You will know the truth, and the truth will set you free"? Well, if truth sets people free, then lies keep them bound. The Enemy's goal is to replace God's truth with deception. This is how it works: A person experiences a painful event such as bullying, betrayal, rejection, church hurt, abuse, divorce, loss, and trauma. The Enemy then whispers a lie. The person hears an internal message that explains their pain, but it's a lie, and they don't know it at the time. Because of this, the person accepts the internal message as truth, and that belief begins to shape their entire outlook on life. Finally, the lie is repeated through life experiences. In other words, the person begins to view every new experience through the lens of that false belief (more on this in step 3). The following table summarizes common lies that begin to take root due to emotional wounds.

THE EMOTIONAL WOUND	THE LIE THAT TAKES ROOT	HOW IT DEVELOPS
Rejection	I am unlovable.	A parent neglects a child, and the Enemy whispers: "You are not worthy of love. No one will ever truly care about you." The child grows up with a fear of relationships and self-sabotages intimacy.
Betrayal	I can't trust anyone.	A spouse or significant other is cheated on, and the Enemy plants the thought: "People will always let you down. You must protect yourself at all costs." Over time, the person withdraws emotionally, refusing to be vulnerable.
Loss	God doesn't care about me.	A woman loses her spouse unexpectedly, and the Enemy whispers, "If God really loved you, He wouldn't have let this happen. You are alone. God has abandoned you." She stops praying and drifts away from God, believing He cannot be trusted.

THE EMOTIONAL WOUND	THE LIE THAT TAKES ROOT	HOW IT DEVELOPS
Failure	I will never be enough.	A man loses his job and struggles financially, and the Enemy reinforces the lie: "You are a failure. Nothing you do will ever succeed." He stops trying for new opportunities, accepting defeat as his identity.
Abuse	I am worthless.	A child grows up in a home with verbal abuse, and over time, they accept the Enemy's lie: "I will never amount to anything. I deserve to be treated this way." Even as an adult, they allow others to mistreat them because they believe they have no value.

This step is extremely dangerous because the person stops questioning whether the lie is true. And once a lie is believed to be true, it's very difficult to break. By the time a lie has taken root, the person is already beginning to build walls of self-protection.

Let's return to Cameron's story. As a result of his Little League experience, these were the lies that Cameron believed about white people:

- All white people are racist deep down.
- White people in authority will always hold me back.
- They will never treat me fairly since they control everything!
- They'll only accept me if I become less "Black" and more "white."
- To be noticed by them, I need to outperform them.
- They're all thinking the same thing my coach said to me.
- I just can't trust a white person.

These lies became deeply embedded within Cameron, and they progressed into the third step.

Step 3: Life confirms the lie

Once a lie has taken root, the person unconsciously filters new experiences through it, further reinforcing the false belief. Over time, every painful event becomes "proof" that the lie is true.

Once again, at this stage, the person no longer questions the lie but expects it to be true. This creates a self-fulfilling cycle, where they unknowingly make choices that strengthen the soul chain rather than break it.

In high school, Cameron tried out for the debate team but was not selected. But he noticed that other white kids were. This rejection reinforced his belief that white people are prejudiced and don't want him to shine.

During his same junior year, he was romantically interested in a white girl with whom he had become good friends. He knew that she was interested in him too. But when he tried to date her, she sadly told him, "I really like you, but my parents won't allow me to date you because you're Black." This reinforced the lies even further.

Cameron went on to major in electrical engineering and was one of the only minorities in his program. He noticed that he was seldom invited to private study groups to help prepare for critical exams. This reinforced the lie he already believed: They don't want me to succeed.

When he landed his first corporate job after college, his colleagues would make statements like, "You're really articulate! Like, you don't even sound Black at all." Or, when they found out what school he attended, they would say things like, "Well, did you get a basketball scholarship or what?" With each microaggression, the lies went deeper and deeper.

Let's examine how this works with the same five lies from the previous step.

THE LIE THAT TOOK ROOT	HOW LIFE REINFORCES THE LIE	THE RESULT
I am unlovable. (Rejection)	A person experiences another relational disappointment, and instead of seeing it as a one-time event, they believe it's further proof that no one will ever love them.	They withdraw from relationships, pushing people away before they can be rejected again.
I can't trust anyone. (Betrayal)	A person shares something personal; when a friend fails to respond ideally, they take it as proof that people will always let them down.	They become emotionally guarded, never allowing deep relationships to form.

God doesn't care about me. (Loss)	After another hardship, they conclude, "God could have stopped this, but He didn't." This becomes further proof that God is distant and uninterested in their pain.	They stop praying, reading Scripture, or trusting God, reinforcing spiritual disconnection.
I will never be enough. (Failure)	They experience a setback at work, school, or in a relationship. Instead of seeing it as an isolated challenge, they believe the lie: "This always happens to me."	They stop trying to improve or take risks, ensuring continued failure.
I am worthless. (Abuse)	Any criticism or rejection (even constructive feedback) reinforces the belief that they deserve mistreatment.	They remain in unhealthy relationships, believing they don't deserve better.

At this stage, the person has enough life evidence to fully embrace the lie as absolute truth. They begin to see proof of this lie everywhere. Each new negative experience they have related to their trauma further embeds the lie within them, reinforcing the soul chain. This leads them to begin interpreting every new situation through the lens of the deeply ingrained lie.

Step 4: Self-protection takes over

By this stage, the lie has been reinforced so often that the person sees it as an undeniable truth. In response, they begin to build emotional walls to protect themselves from further pain. While these walls may feel like a form of self-preservation, they actually strengthen the soul chain, preventing the person from experiencing healing, meaningful relationships, and spiritual freedom.

Let's review how this worked in Cameron's life.

The Wound: When Cameron was ten, his Little League coach made racist comments and consistently mistreated him compared to his white teammates. That moment planted the wound of rejection and inferiority, explicitly tied to race.

The Lie: All white people are against me. They will never see me as an equal.

The Reinforcement: In high school, he was overlooked for starting positions in basketball while less talented white players got more playing time. Then his white love interest told him that her white parents would never accept him. And on the job his ideas were brushed aside while microaggressions from coworkers confirmed the suspicion that he wasn't entirely accepted.

The Wall: Over time, Cameron began to build a wall of self-protection. He refused to trust white authority figures, keeping them at a distance. He worked twice as hard to prove himself, but even success didn't silence the suspicion. He stopped trying to form close relationships with white colleagues, convinced that doing so would only open him to more pain.

The Bondage: What began as a defense mechanism became a prison. Cameron's wall kept out the sting of rejection, but it also blocked him from potential friendships, partnerships, and opportunities for healing. He felt justified in his mistrust but found himself isolated and exhausted.

The Result: Instead of freeing him, Cameron's wall of self-protection reinforced the bitterness inside him. The very thing he thought would keep him safe was actually keeping him bound.

Step 5: The lie becomes identity

At this final stage, the lie is no longer just a belief; it has become part of the person's identity. They no longer say, "I struggle with this." Instead, they say, "This is who I am."

What began as a painful event and became a deceptive thought, reinforced by experiences and protected by walls of self-defense, has now entirely shaped how the person views life as a whole. At this point, breaking free feels difficult and impossible because they cannot imagine life outside of their accepted identity.

To illustrate this, we will return to Cameron's story. As the lie further took root, Cameron fully embraced a victim mentality. Instead of believing lies about white people, he believed lies about himself.

- I can't change my future because I'll always be held back.
- I'm limited in what I can achieve because the system is rigged against me.
- I'll never be as good as my white peers, no matter how hard I work.
- I'll always be overlooked, so there's really no point in trying to work harder.

At this stage Cameron no longer saw these as *thoughts* but as *truths about who he was*. Instead of believing, "People mistreat me," he thought. "I am inherently less, powerless, disadvantaged." This is precisely how a soul chain becomes identity, shaping not just a person's beliefs but their entire outlook, decisions, and relationships.

Here are some other examples.

ORIGINAL WOUND	LIE ACCEPTED AS TRUTH	SOUL CHAIN BECOMES IDENTITY
A child grows up feeling unseen and ignored.	I am unimportant and invisible.	I am just a background person—I have nothing valuable to offer.
A woman was deeply betrayed in a relationship.	No one can be trusted.	I am someone who will always be alone.
A man grows up hearing he is stupid and will never succeed.	I will always be a failure..	I am a failure. Nothing I do will ever matter.
A person experiences trauma and fear at a young age.	The world is unsafe. I must always be on guard.	I am an anxious person. I will never be at peace.

Open emotional wounds can be some of the most deceptive seeds for soul chains because they feel justified. After all, no one chooses to be hurt, rejected, betrayed, abandoned, or abused.

I feel like this would be a great place to pause and remind you that God's intent was never for us to be defined by our emotional wounds. Stay with me, because in future chapters, we will explore how to experience healing and freedom so that these soul chains can be broken in our lives.

So far, we've discussed how soul chains are formed through lies, sinful patterns, and emotional wounds. However, there is one final way in which soul chains are formed, which often goes unnoticed but is highly relevant to the times in which we live. And that is cultural influences. Before you ask, "How can our culture create a soul chain in my life?" remember the first part of our definition of a soul chain: "A soul chain is a deeply entrenched mindset." Culture can create deeply entrenched mindsets that oppose God's truth.

Sadly, most people don't even realize that culture is shaping them. Because we are so inundated with what our culture believes, many of us accept it as truth without even questioning it.

Let's explore precisely how this happens.

Soul Chains Are Formed Through Cultural Influences

The Enemy uses our culture to expose messages that oppose a Christian worldview. At first these messages may seem harmless, intriguing, or even good. Remember, in the garden, Satan's strategy was to create doubt. Genesis 3:1 says, "The serpent said to the woman, 'Did God really say . . . ?'" (my paraphrase). And this is what he is doing today. He wants people to doubt God, Christianity, and God's Word.

Here are some modern examples of cultural ideas that can turn into soul chains.

CULTURAL MESSAGE INTRODUCED	HOW IT BEGINS	WHERE IT LEADS
Follow your heart.	Promoted in movies, music, and self-help culture	Leads to self-led morality rather than biblical obedience

CULTURAL MESSAGE INTRODUCED	HOW IT BEGINS	WHERE IT LEADS
Your truth is what matters.	Taught in education, media, and self-empowerment trends	Leads to relativism, where there is no absolute truth
Sexual freedom equals happiness.	Promoted in entertainment, celebrity culture, and activism	Leads to immorality, shame, broken relationships, and identity confusion
Happiness is life's highest goal.	Reinforced in social media, advertising, and lifestyle branding	Leads to self-centered living rather than godly purpose
Christianity is oppressive.	Taught in universities, entertainment, and progressive movements	Leads to the deconstruction of faith and rejection of biblical authority

Wow! Does this not sum up our culture today? At this stage, the idea is not yet a soul chain, but it has been introduced, and if left unchallenged, it will begin to shape thinking.

Normalization comes next. This is where the belief or idea transitions from being merely an option to an expectation. What was once questioned, debated, and possibly rejected becomes part of the cultural mainstream. It becomes less shocking, and people stop questioning it over time.

A great example of this is how entertainment has essentially normalized immorality. Recently my wife and I were watching a show together, and we were *really* into it. Every episode had us on the edge of our seats. The storyline was fantastic. The character development was amazing. And the cliffhangers had us bingeing for hours. We even began to tell our friends about the show. And then it happened. Halfway into the first season, one of the female characters became sexually involved with another female. The particular scene and the ones that ensued due to this new development made it extremely uncomfortable for us to continue watching together. And it certainly made it more difficult to recommend the show to others. We said to each other, "Why does it seem like just about every show we watch is trying to push the LGBTQ+ agenda forward?" The reason is that the media wants to normalize it. What was once considered shocking in movies and TV is now expected, embraced, and celebrated.

This is how it works. It begins with familiarity. You are bombarded with messages through various media, including government, social media, and education. Next, it becomes expected. If you don't get on board with this idea, you are labeled as intolerant or "old-fashioned." After this, it becomes institutionalized. This is where schools, corporations, and governments enforce policies that embed this belief (idea) into our everyday lives. Then it becomes morally defended. The culture begins to protect the lie as if it were a moral cause, making opposition to it seem evil. Finally, biblical truth is vilified. Those who challenge the belief are labeled as bigots, extremists, or even enemies of progress. In other words, if you don't agree with these ideas, *you* are not progressing and are trying to keep our culture stuck in the Stone Age.

This is where the soul chain begins. Since the culture now accepts this idea as gospel truth, individuals internalize these lies and begin to see them as personal truths or rights. It becomes their identity. The belief becomes deeply ingrained in their worldview, shaping their reality, identity, decisions, values, and lives. What was once merely an outside influence is now an internal conviction. They don't question it; instead, they defend it and even teach it to others. They no longer even consider the possibility that they could be wrong. Any attempt to challenge their belief or lifestyle is met with anger, resistance, defensiveness, or dismissal. They become an ambassador for the cultural lie, convinced their mission is to help others experience this newfound freedom. The soul chain is formed because the individual feels as though this mindset or habit is either unnecessary or impossible to break.

Do you see a pattern among the different ways these soul chains are formed? Each of them seeks to hijack a person's identity and convince them to believe they are someone other than who God created them to be.

Conclusion

Whether you relate to Linda, Brett, Cameron, or one of the biblical characters, the reality remains: There is a soul chain in your life that needs to be broken. Since they are not formed overnight, they will more than likely not be broken overnight. As we move through this book together, please remain hopeful. Remember the promise of freedom that awaits you. Remember that Jesus didn't just die to forgive you of your sin. He died so that you could experience true freedom: freedom in your mind, your relationships, your identity, and your purpose.

Whatever has kept you bound does not have to define you. It doesn't matter how long you've carried the lie. It doesn't matter how deep the pain of your trauma is. It doesn't matter how strong that addiction is. These soul chains can be broken. That's the power of the cross.

As we turn the page, I invite you to not only learn about soul chains but also begin identifying them in your own life. Remember, awareness is not failure. On the contrary, it's the doorway that leads to your freedom.

So breathe, and keep going, knowing that the same Jesus who rose from the dead is the One who has already given you resurrection power through His Spirit.

REFLECTION QUESTIONS

1. What deeply entrenched belief, habit, or mindset in your life might be opposing God's truth, even if it currently feels "normal" or justifiable?

2. Are there lies you've believed about God, yourself, or your worth that have shaped how you think, behave, or relate to others?

3. Have you noticed any repeated sin patterns in your life that may have started small but now feel difficult, or even impossible, to break?

4. Can you identify a painful experience (emotional wound) from your past that may have led you to adopt a false belief about yourself or God?

5. In what areas of your life do you tend to justify unhealthy or sinful behavior? What excuses or internal dialogues do you use to rationalize them?

6. Have cultural messages or trends influenced your thinking in ways that conflict with biblical truth? If so, where have you seen those ideas take root in your identity or worldview?

7. Do you find yourself defining who you are by your struggle, sin, or wounds instead of by your identity in Christ? If so, what would it look like to begin challenging that belief?

CHAPTER 2

SIX CHAINS THAT BIND THE SOUL

A really close friend of mine shared her story with me years ago, and it nearly broke my heart. For privacy purposes, we will refer to her as Anna. She never saw herself as very attractive. In middle school and high school, she rarely got attention from guys and constantly compared herself to other "more attractive" girls. So she figured she would get attention in a different way. She began to dress provocatively, showcasing her body through her attire.

Anna quickly noticed that she finally got the attention she'd always wanted. But it wasn't the proper attention. The boys only gave her attention because they assumed she was easy and could be taken advantage of. Deep down, she knew this was the wrong type of attention, but in her mind, some attention was better than no attention at all. As the attention started pouring in, it became increasingly more difficult for her to maintain her purity, and eventually she gave in. Because she was empty emotionally, the attention she received from being physically involved with guys filled a hole she didn't even know she had. Her promiscuous behavior continued, and by the time she graduated from college, she had slept with twenty-two men.

But something radical happened to her shortly after graduation. Jesus found her and saved her. She quickly made a vow of celibacy. She knew her worth and was committed to living her life for her newfound Savior. She then attended seminary. She met a great Christian guy, and they began dating. Things started getting serious pretty quickly, and she was over the moon about the possibility of marrying this wonderful Christian man.

But then he asked her the question she'd hoped no man would ever ask: "How many men have you been with?" Anna had a decision to make. She thought, "I could lie, but I'm a Christian and I know God would not be pleased." Additionally, "If I lie and he later discovers the truth, he might resent marrying me and feel deceived. I should tell him the truth." She mustered up the courage to tell him the truth. "I've slept with twenty-two men," she said. And what happened next devastated her. To her shock and utter disbelief, he said that since he was a virgin, he wasn't able to get over her having been with that many men. He said he would constantly be comparing himself to the men she'd been with, and it was too much for him. Despite trying her best to convince him that she wasn't interested in any of those other men and that she never loved them, he simply was not able to look past it and broke off the relationship. She was shell-shocked. "Jesus," she cried, "I committed myself to celibacy. I told the truth. I thought I was forgiven. Why did this happen?" And from that moment forward, a soul chain of shame began to wrap itself around her as she bought into the lie that she would never be fully known and fully loved at the same time.

Perhaps you can relate to Anna's story. Her soul chain was shame, but there are many different types of soul chains, and in this chapter, we will define, describe, and identify six primary categories. They are spiritual, emotional, generational, sexual, relational, and psychological. Each one operates slightly differently, but the end goal the Enemy has for all of them is the same: to keep people bound so they don't experience freedom and walk in victory. I'm warning you ahead of time that this chapter may be the most difficult one to read because it is going to force you to go places you may not want to go. It will challenge you to explore areas of your heart that you may not have explored before. My goal for you is that by the end of this chapter, you will be able to clearly identify what soul chains may be strengthening their grip on you so that we can dismantle them one by one.

Soul Chain 1: Spiritual Soul Chains

A spiritual soul chain is a false belief about God, spiritual matters, or the unseen realm that keeps a person from fully trusting, obeying, or experiencing God. At their core, these types of soul chains are designed to *create a false image of God*. God is harsh, mean, angry, distant, unconcerned, unloving, weak, or even nonexistent. The Enemy's goal is to replace truth with tradition, opinions, or deception. The goal is to encourage the individual to elevate their personal views, feelings, or beliefs to a level of authority equal to or greater than that of the Word of God. Let's examine two of them and how they manifest in our lives.

The Soul Chain of Rational Thought

A rational soul chain is a mindset that elevates human reason, logic, or scientific understanding above the authority of God's Word. It is resistant to spiritual truth unless it can be fully explained, proven, or understood through natural means.

Earlier, we established a connection between soul chains and a more commonly known term: a stronghold. I believe this was the primary application in Paul's day when he wrote 2 Corinthians 10:4–5: "The weapons we fight with are not the weapons of the world. On the contrary, they have divine power to demolish strongholds [soul chains]. We demolish arguments and every pretension that sets itself up against the knowledge of God, and we take captive every thought to make it obedient to Christ."

The Greek word used in this passage for "argument" is *logismos*, which refers primarily to reasoned thoughts, conclusions, or arguments, especially those built on human reasoning.[1] When Paul wrote this, certain mindsets were deeply ingrained in the culture that hindered people from accepting the truth about Jesus.

In Paul's time, many people didn't reject the gospel because of a lack of evidence; instead, it was because they were already captive to well-developed philosophical systems that shaped their understanding of truth, life, and even the divine. These systems acted as rational soul chains, creating intellectual pride and spiritual blindness that resisted the message of Christ. First, there was *Greek philosophy and intellectualism*. At the time, Athens was the intellectual hub of the ancient world, and Greek philosophy dominated the minds of the people. Paul encountered this when he ministered in Athens. While he was waiting for Timothy and Silas to join him there, we read in Acts 17:16 that "he was deeply troubled by all the idols he saw everywhere in the city" (NLT).

Right away, we see that Paul was ministering in a context that did not accept the truth that there is one true God. It goes on to say in verses 17–18, "He went to the synagogue to reason with the Jews and the God-fearing Gentiles, and he spoke daily in the public square to all who happened to be there. He also had a debate with Epicurean and Stoic philosophers. When he told them about Jesus and his resurrection, they said, 'What's this babbler trying to say with these strange ideas he's picked up?' Others said, 'He seems to be preaching about some foreign gods.'"

This is a perfect illustration of the type of thinking present within Paul's culture. I encourage you to read the remainder of the chapter to see how Paul confronted these false beliefs about God.

Another popular false belief in Paul's time was *Gnosticism*. People who followed this belief thought that everything physical, such as the body or the material world, was inherently bad or flawed. Because of that, they refused to believe that Jesus could have come to earth in a real human body, because to them, God would never lower Himself to take on something as "dirty" as flesh. So they rejected the idea that Jesus was both fully God and fully human.

Then there was *skepticism* and *relativism*. Many in Paul's day had grown disillusioned with the endless debates of philosophers. They turned to the belief that truth is unknowable (meaning it's not possible to know what is true and what is not), or that it's flexible and personal. As you can imagine, this would directly oppose Jesus's claim in John 14:6, "I am the way and the truth and the life. No one comes to the Father except through me."

Finally, there was *idolatry* and *mythology*. The Roman world was filled with gods, temples, and superstitions. Paul pointed this out in his discussion with the philosophers on Mars Hill: "Paul, standing before the council, addressed them as follows: 'Men of Athens, I notice that you are very religious in every way, for as I was walking along I saw your many shrines. And one of your altars had this inscription on it: "To an Unknown God." This God, whom you worship without knowing, is the one I'm telling you about'" (Acts 17:22–23 NLT).

So it was widely accepted that there could not be "one God" with "one truth." In their minds many gods led to a cultural worldview that opposed the Christian worldview. These were just a few of the "arguments" that exalted themselves against the knowledge of God in the first century. Do any of these sound familiar?

While the specific names of these ancient philosophies have changed, sadly, their core ideas are alive and well today, just disguised in new language. These modern "arguments" or rational soul chains form powerful mental barriers that keep many people from receiving the truth about God and His Word. They are very subtle because most of them don't sound at all hostile or demonic. They actually make sense to most people, which is the problem. At their root, they elevate human understanding above divine revelation, making it impossible to walk by faith.

One of the most common rational soul chains is *scientific naturalism*. This is the belief that reality is limited to what can be observed, measured, or proven through the scientific method. In other words, something can't be trusted if it can't be seen under a microscope or demonstrated in a lab. A college science professor, for instance, might confidently say, "I will only believe in what science can prove." But the gospel story isn't something that can be proven in a science lab; it's a supernatural truth that must be accepted by faith.

Another rational soul chain is the *overreliance on logic and reason* as the final authority. Biblical faith often requires people to trust beyond what they can calculate or understand.

When filtering everything through the lens of human logic and reason, the gospel is rejected as foolishness (1 Corinthians 1:18). An atheist like Richard Dawkins might say, "I just can't believe in something that doesn't make sense to me." However, God's Word states that His ways are higher than ours and His thoughts are higher than our thoughts, implying that His wisdom cannot always be understood by logic (Isaiah 55:8–9).

Closely related is *philosophical skepticism* (similar to what was seen in Paul's day), which resists the idea that we can know absolute truth at all. A new age spiritual person might say, "Who really knows what's true? Everyone sees things differently." This attitude sounds open-minded, but in reality, it shuts the door on the absolute truth of Scripture and the exclusive claims of Christ. This is perhaps one of the most popular barriers to faith in our society today.

Moral relativism is particularly dominant in our culture today. This is the idea that truth is personal and subjective, not objective. What's right for you may not be right for me. In this worldview, sin is redefined as personal choice, and accountability becomes offensive. A progressive Christian who rejects absolute truth may say something like, "That might be wrong for you, but I don't see anything wrong with it." This erodes the moral foundation of the gospel, which declares that all have sinned and fall short of God's glory (Romans 3:23). This also erodes the idea that Scripture should be the final authority by which we govern our lives.

Finally, there's the rational soul chain of *intellectual pride*. This is evident in individuals who place great confidence in their education, intelligence, or ability to reason. To them, faith feels like weakness or wishful thinking. An atheist might say, "I've studied all the religions; Christianity just doesn't hold up intellectually." The gospel challenges this mindset by reminding us that God's wisdom often confounds the so-called wisdom of the world (1 Corinthians 1:27).

On the surface, these rational soul chains may sound different, but they all have one thing in common: Human thought is elevated above divine truth, which is why Paul commanded us Christians in 2 Corinthians 10:5 to "demolish arguments and every pretension that sets itself up against the knowledge of God, and . . . take captive every thought to make it obedient to Christ."

In 2 Corinthians 4:4, Paul said that what's happening behind the scenes is that "the God of this age has blinded the minds of unbelievers, so that they cannot see the light of the gospel that displays the glory of Christ, who is the image of God."

Satan is actively working to blind the minds of those who don't believe by elevating these worldly "arguments," or rational soul chains. The church must be vigilant to "pull them down" and "destroy them" as Paul commanded.

The Soul Chain of Legalism

If rational-thought soul chains primarily influence nonbelievers (and some believers), the spiritual soul chain of legalism primarily affects believers. This is a prevalent soul chain that many Christians are unaware they are bound by. Legalism is a performance-based approach to faith where a person believes that their standing with God is determined by their ability to follow a set of rules, rituals, or traditions.

Legalism replaces grace with works and shifts the focus from what Christ has done for us to what we need to do for Him to earn His approval. It creates a distorted view of God where we begin to see Him as a harsh taskmaster who is angry with us and will remain so until we adhere to a set of rituals with near perfection. It fosters a fear-based relationship with God and often accompanies feelings of guilt and self-righteousness. A sign that this may be a soul chain in your life is if you believe that God loves you more when you obey Him and less when you don't. This false belief system is based on a misunderstanding of what Christ has done for us on the cross.

God's love for you doesn't depend on what you do but on what Christ has done. Is God displeased when we disobey Him? Yes, of course. But His love does not change.

Another sign of legalism is when you measure your spiritual worth by things like church attendance, how much you read the Bible, or how perfectly you obey God. Or you consistently doubt whether you are saved due to your inability to live up to a standard of perfection.

Additionally, the soul chain of legalism can mean you are often very critical of yourself for falling short of a perfect spiritual standard. Finally, you usually feel unworthy of God's best for your life because you consistently fall short. Ultimately, you often find yourself judging others in the same way you believe God judges you. This may include feeling spiritually superior to people who engage in certain activities you think are off-limits but are not explicitly condemned in Scripture.

The Pharisees are the perfect example of a group of people bound by the soul chain of legalism. And, as with other soul chains, they didn't even realize it. They created a set of man-made rules and expected everyone else to follow them.

We see this clearly in Mark 7, when the Pharisees confronted Jesus because His disciples didn't follow their traditional hand-washing rituals. Jesus responded by exposing the heart of their legalism. Verses 8 and 13 say, "You have let go of the commands of God and are holding on to human traditions. . . . You nullify the word of God by your tradition that you have handed down."

The Pharisees had elevated their rules over a relationship with God. Tradition was often more valued than truth, as people became more concerned with appearances than with genuine obedience to God. The worst part about this was that they were convinced they were doing it right. This is the inherent danger of legalism as a soul chain: It appears righteous, but it's rooted in pride, control, and fear.

Soul Chain 2: Emotional Soul Chains

While spiritual soul chains center around a distorted view of God, emotional soul chains are feelings-based mindsets that shape how a person sees themselves and others. Let's explore several of these so you can identify them in your life.

The Soul Chain of Shame

Shame can be described as a deep sense of unworthiness, guilt, or self-condemnation that makes a person feel permanently damaged, unlovable, or beyond God's forgiveness. This was what my friend Anna was wrestling with. It was also what Linda was wrestling with because of her guilt and embarrassment over her daughter's suicide.

You believe that God has forgiven others, but He certainly can't forgive you for what you've done. Shame tries to convince you that you are disqualified from receiving God's best and maybe even disqualified from receiving love from God and others. Shame whispers, "No one could truly love me if they knew what I've done or what has been done to me." Shame causes you to refrain from engaging in intimate relationships, fearing you wouldn't be fully loved if you were fully known. You may even hesitate to pray or worship because you don't feel worthy. Shame also causes you to view every negative situation in your life as a possible punishment for past sins and failures.

The Soul Chain of Fear

Fear is a natural and oftentimes healthy emotion. But when a person is controlled by fear, it becomes a soul chain. Unlike healthy fear, which warns of real danger, a soul chain of fear is rooted in deception. It convinces people that the worst will happen, that they are powerless, and that God cannot be trusted. Fear can manifest itself in several ways. There is fear of failure that says, "I can't try this because I'll mess it up." This is when a person is so afraid of trying something that they've convinced themselves it won't work and will result in failure. So they live their lives safe within their comfort zone. There is also the fear of rejection, which says, "If I open up, they'll reject me." It leads a person to avoid forming deep relationships out of fear of being hurt or rejected by others. Then there's the fear of the future, which says, "What if everything goes wrong?" A person in bondage to this fear continually plays the what-if game. They believe in the worst-case scenario and obsess over things before they even happen. And there is the fear of abandonment, which says, "Everyone always leaves me." This person is convinced that everyone eventually leaves them, no matter what. Finally, there is the fear of death, which says, "Something bad is going to happen to me or my family."

When I started my YouTube channel in 2015, I faced many of the same fears that others have.

- What if people don't think my videos are good?
- What if I'm unable to learn what I need to know to produce good videos?
- How will I deal with online criticism?
- What if I don't have the time to create videos consistently?

- What if people attack my beliefs?
- What if I don't have the correct responses when people criticize my content?
- What if we don't have enough money for equipment and to hire people to help?
- What if I become an even bigger target for the Enemy because I put myself out there?

I would be lying to you if I didn't admit that I had all of those thoughts. However, the difference between being afraid and being controlled by fear lies in having the courage to do what God has called you to do, despite your fears. Looking back over many years, I can hardly imagine what my life would be like today if I had allowed fear to dominate it. Yet many people never reach the other side of their dreams because they allow the soul chain of fear to paralyze them.

The Soul Chain of Anger

Similar to fear, anger is a God-given emotion that is also healthy. Even God gets angry. The Bible actually commands us to be angry, but not to sin in our anger (Ephesians 4:26–27). The anger we are discussing here is when it is misplaced, unresolved, and uncontrollable, ultimately resulting in damaged relationships.

A soul chain of anger is not just about getting frustrated occasionally; it's a deeper issue. It's a deep-seated pattern of resentment, bitterness, or hostility that controls a person's reactions. It can be triggered by past wounds, betrayal, disappointments, or perceived injustices, causing a person to live in a state of offense, rage, or silent resentment (more on this later).

Anger manifests itself in frequent, explosive outbursts that may involve rage, yelling, aggression, or even physical abuse. It often results from a short temper, where small things cause significant reactions. The individual may feel guilty afterward, but they struggle to change.

A person can even manifest anger by being angry with God. They may feel abandoned by God and question why He allowed certain things to happen in their life, leaving them in a state of anger and thus separating them from the intimacy God desires in our relationship with Him. Finally, anger can be self-directed, where people are constantly angry at themselves. I'm reminded of the quote, "Holding on to anger is like grasping a hot coal with the intent of throwing it at someone else; you are the one who gets burned." These are wise words to keep in mind when struggling with anger.

The Soul Chain of Unforgiveness

Closely connected to anger is the soul chain of unforgiveness. When a person refuses to forgive, they unknowingly give the Enemy (and others, for that matter) a foothold in their heart, allowing wounds to fester and grow into deeper spiritual, emotional, and relational damage.

Instead of moving forward in freedom, unforgiveness keeps an individual attached to their pain because they are constantly reliving offenses and rehearsing past wrongs. Over time, this soul chain affects attitudes, relationships, and even physical health, as studies have shown that bitterness and unforgiveness can lead to stress, anxiety, and other health issues.[2]

Unforgiveness can manifest itself in several ways. At times, it looks like holding on to offenses. It's when a person mentally says, "I'll forgive you, but I will never forget what you've done." Obviously, it's impossible to forget the pain someone has caused, but this mentality keeps them tethered to the painful experience. They find themselves repeatedly bringing up wrongs, even long after the offense has occurred. Whenever they think of the person or situation, their blood boils again as anger and resentment resurface. This ultimately keeps them in an emotional cycle that prevents healing and restoration.

Unforgiveness can manifest itself in an insatiable desire for revenge or justice. Revenge is when we take matters into our own hands to try to even the scales for what was done to us. Justice is when we secretly hope God punishes an individual for what they've done, so they can feel the same level of pain and hurt they caused us to feel. We feel satisfied when they experience hardship. Instead of seeking healing, we hold on to the hope that the person who hurt us will suffer in return. Consequently, we cannot pray for our offender's well-being because our bitterness overshadows our ability to show mercy and extend grace.

Another hazardous effect of unforgiveness is a hard heart. Unforgiveness can cause a person to secretly believe the lie: "I can't trust people anymore." They become guarded, cynical, and closed off in relationships, refusing to allow themselves to be truly vulnerable again. However, they don't realize that the Enemy uses their desire to protect themselves from further harm as a weapon against them, isolating them even more. Speaking of isolation, unforgiveness and bitterness cause people to go out of their way to avoid situations where they might have to interact with the person who hurt them, but in doing so, they also prevent opportunities for reconciliation and peace.

Finally, bitterness and unforgiveness can hinder a person from experiencing healthy relationships. Someone struggling with unforgiveness may say to themself, "I don't want to get close to anyone." They will unknowingly allow their past hurts to dictate how they treat new people. Instead of giving others a fair chance, they assume that everyone will eventually hurt or betray them just as someone else did. This leads to deep loneliness, as walls built to protect from pain also block love, trust, and meaningful relationships.

One clear case of how bitterness and unforgiveness can become soul chains in our lives is the story of Jacob and Esau. You may recall that in Genesis 25, Esau was hunting in the field and came home famished. Have you ever been so hungry that all you could think about was your next meal? Esau must have felt this way because he asked his brother, Jacob, if he could have some of the red stew that he was making. Now, if Jacob hadn't been such a selfish trickster, he would have just given his brother some stew. Instead, Jacob saw this as an opportunity to exploit his brother's hunger for his gain. Essentially, he said, "Sure, I'll give you some stew . . . in exchange for your birthright."

Now, a birthright may not sound significant to us, but it was a monumental thing in that culture. You see, the birthright was an extraordinary inheritance given by the father to the firstborn son. For example, if the father had three sons, instead of dividing the inheritance into three equal portions, the firstborn would receive two-thirds of the inheritance, and the other two sons would split the remaining one-third. The son with the birthright would be seen as the official leader of the family after the father's passing. He would be responsible for making key decisions for the family and caring for them. More specifically, for Jacob and Esau, it meant that Jacob would receive the covenantal promises from God. So instead of Abraham, Isaac, and Esau, it now became Abraham, Isaac, and Jacob. So yeah, it was a big thing!

The fact that Jacob would take advantage of Esau's hunger infuriated him, and he felt betrayed. But that is not where the betrayal ends. In Genesis 27, toward the end of Isaac's life, he was no longer able to see well, and he wanted one last good meal. Not gonna lie, that's probably what I would have asked for too. He told his son Esau to go out into the country, find some game for him, and come back and cook his favorite meal. Well, Esau did what his father asked him to do. In the meantime, back at home, because Rebekah favored Jacob over Esau, she saw a deceptive way in which Jacob could receive his father's blessing instead of Esau. She quickly whipped up her husband's favorite meal and told Jacob to go and give it to him. Jacob knew his father would soon realize it was he, not Esau, who was bringing him the meal. So Rebekah covered Jacob in goatskins so his skin would feel hairy like Esau's. When Jacob took the meal to his father, Isaac, despite his doubt, blessed Jacob, thinking it was Esau. This was significant because in that culture, words had power. Isaac's words were essentially legally binding, like a contract. He even said in the story that he couldn't take it back. It was irreversible. Isaac conferred on Jacob both material and spiritual wealth, leadership and authority over Esau, covenantal favor, and divine protection.

Sadly, when Esau returned and realized that Jacob had stolen his blessing, Isaac explained the seriousness of the blessing. He said to Esau, "I have made Jacob your master and have declared that all his brothers will be his servants. I have guaranteed him an abundance of grain and wine—what is left for me to give you, my son?" (Genesis 27:37 NLT).

Then we have one of the most poignant scenes in all of Scripture. It says in verse 38, "Esau pleaded, 'But do you have only one blessing? Oh my father, bless me, too!' Then Esau broke down and wept."

I can just imagine how angry Esau was at this point. First he was deceived into selling his birthright, and now Jacob had stolen his blessing. The Bible says that Esau was so angry that he wanted to kill his brother (verse 41). Jacob had to be sent away to be kept safe.

For twenty years, their relationship was severed. Jacob lived in exile, carrying the weight of his deceit, while Esau harbored deep bitterness. Their estrangement was marked by unforgiveness: one brother living in guilt, the other in resentment. But when the time came for Jacob to return home, he feared Esau's wrath. So he sent extravagant gifts ahead as peace offerings, hoping to appease his brother (32:3–21).

Yet when Esau saw Jacob, he did not seek revenge; he forgave. Instead of striking his brother down, he ran to meet him, embraced him, and wept (33:4). The soul chain of bitterness that had fueled Esau's hatred for years was broken in that moment of forgiveness and reconciliation.

I've always taken pride in being able to forgive others. That is, until I was deeply hurt by a spiritual leader many years ago. Many hurtful things were said to me by this man. I also felt he intentionally tried to hinder me from thriving in ministry. I continued to attend the church for years afterward, but I could tell that I hadn't forgiven him because

I was thoroughly checked out from his sermons on Sunday mornings. When I heard him preach each week, something within me cringed, making it nearly impossible for me to receive spiritual truth from him. I experienced most of the signs I discussed previously. I was bitter, but I eventually came to terms with the situation when I truly extended forgiveness to him. To this day I still feel the pain of what was said, but my bitterness toward the man is gone.

An important distinction needs to be made here regarding forgiveness: Forgiveness is not the absence of pain but the absence of bitterness.

I devoted more time to this specific soul chain because the Enemy often uses it to keep many believers bound. Sadly, there are many Christians who go their entire lives bitter at something that happened to them many years ago.

Before we move on, I want to invite you to truly ask yourself, "Who do I need to forgive today? Who am I still bitter toward?" Maybe it's an old friend you haven't spoken to in a while. Maybe it's a family member or a colleague at work. Maybe it's someone you had a sharp disagreement with and decided to part ways. Search your heart. Ask God to show you who you need to extend forgiveness to, and then ask Him for the courage to do so.

Soul Chain 3: Generational Soul Chains

If you've been around Christian circles for any length of time, you've undoubtedly heard of the term *generational curses*. Because Christians cannot be under a curse, I'd like to suggest an alternate name: generational soul chains. These could be patterns of sin, destructive behaviors, or even harmful mindsets that are passed down from one generation to the next. If these are not addressed, they will continue to impact future generations. As we go through these, consider which ones you may have been exposed to in your family of origin.

The Soul Chain of Addiction

Addiction can cover anything from gambling to overeating to substance abuse (alcohol, drugs) to workaholism, as well as any compulsive behaviors passed down through family cycles. You've probably heard the saying that more is caught than taught. This means that much of what we do today was not formally taught to us. We observed it happening around us, becoming a part of how we function.

Identifying whether something is an addiction or not is a key step to experiencing victory. Here are several helpful and practical indicators:

- **Lack of control:** You've tried to stop multiple times but can't.
- **Consuming thoughts:** You're always thinking about it, even when you're not doing it.
- **Negative consequences:** It's hurting your relationships, health, or relationship with God, yet you continue to do it anyway.
- **Secrecy:** You're hiding it from others because of shame or guilt.
- **Emotional dependency:** You turn to it to cope with stress, loneliness, or emotional pain.

If you're experiencing any of these indicators, you may be wrestling with an addiction of some sort that needs to be brought into the light.

The Soul Chain of Poverty Mindset

This occurs when a pattern of financial struggle arises from a lack of financial stewardship, a fear of financial responsibility, or the belief that financial freedom and prosperity are unattainable or undeserved. In some situations, the person can even fear financial success or feel guilty if they are blessed financially. They adopt the mindset that perhaps God wants them to be poor. They view money as evil, fearing it will corrupt them. Or, even if they are financially comfortable, they always worry that they will somehow run out of money and struggle to enjoy what God has blessed them with. They pass down habits of debt, poor money management, or a fear of financial success.

Here are some helpful ways to identify a poverty mindset.

- You often feel like there is never enough, even when your needs are met.
- You live with a perpetual fear that you're one step away from being broke.
- You feel guilty when you make a substantial purchase (constant buyer's remorse).
- You grew up in a family where financial struggles were seen as "just the way it is."
- You avoid financial planning, budgeting, or taking steps to improve your financial situation.
- You assume you'll always be in debt, so why even try to pay it off?
- You struggle to give money to others for fear that you won't have enough left for yourself.
- You feel guilty or unworthy of financial success or abundance.
- You struggle with impulsive spending or fear of making wise investments.
- You often speak negatively about money, believing it is impossible to ever achieve financial freedom.

This is a soul chain that I still wrestle with today. When my parents got divorced in 1981, my sister and I stayed with my mother. She taught elementary deaf children for thirty-four years. Although she worked extremely hard to provide for our family, I knew even at a young age that finances were tight for us. On my father's side, it was the same way.

I'll never forget when I spent summers with my grandparents and we would go to a fast-food drive-through. I'd order a cheeseburger and my grandfather would say, "You don't need to order a cheeseburger! Order a hamburger! We've got cheese at home. I'm not paying twenty-six cents for a piece of cheese." So when we got home, he'd take out a large piece of frozen government cheese, slice it unevenly, and slap that unmelted piece on my hamburger and it became a cheeseburger! I grew up with this mentality that money was something I needed to hold on to tightly because if I didn't, it could disappear, and then I wouldn't have enough to provide for myself.

I didn't realize just how much this soul chain had dominated my thinking until I got married in 2015. My wife didn't grow up with that mentality, so she viewed money totally differently. When we got married, she wanted to travel and "enjoy life." I was always worried that if we spent money on a vacation, we might not have enough money to get out of debt or for other "more important" things. So we struggled to compromise in this area. Sometimes when we went out, my wife would want a bottle of water that cost five dollars. Yes, I would get it for her because I try to be a good husband; however, in the back of my mind, a poverty mindset still lingered. What if we keep wasting money on things like bottled water and one day run out of money?

I deceived myself into thinking, "Well, when we get to a better place financially, I'll be more willing to spend money." But sadly, that didn't happen. I still cringe at paying five dollars for bottled water! As a matter of fact, I'm in a hotel room right now writing this book, and in my room there were two smaller bottles of complimentary water and one larger bottle for five dollars. I did not drink the five-dollar bottle but drank the two free ones!

My wife still loves to give money away, and I'm still a bit tight, constantly worrying that if we give it away, our needs won't be met. Not only does this soul chain hinder me from enjoying what God has blessed me with, but it also causes me to be extremely stingy, which is antithetical to being generous. But this deeply entrenched mindset was inherently passed down to me from previous generations.

The Soul Chain of Dysfunctional Relationships

This soul chain occurs when cycles of broken marriages or unhealthy family dynamics persist across multiple generations. It could be repeated patterns of divorce, unhealthy and toxic communication patterns, emotional neglect, or a failure to resolve conflicts in a healthy and godly way, leading to generational wounds in relationships. As I mentioned in detail in the preface, this was the primary generational soul chain I was determined to break, and by the power of God, I did. Here are a few practical ways to identify this soul chain.

- You find yourself in a cycle of unhealthy dating or marriage relationships, repeating the same toxic patterns.
- You have difficulty trusting your partner due to past experiences or generational wounds.
- Arguments often escalate into destructive conflict rather than healthy resolution.
- You feel emotionally disconnected or struggle with intimacy in relationships.
- Your relationships are marked by manipulation, control, or codependency.
- You grew up seeing dysfunction in marriages and relationships, and now you struggle to build a healthy one yourself.
- You often sabotage relationships by seeking perfection out of fear of being hurt.
- You attract or pursue partners who exhibit the same toxic traits you witnessed growing up.
- There is a pattern of infidelity, abandonment, or broken commitments in your family history.

One of my favorite scriptures concerning generational soul chains that is often misinterpreted is Exodus 20:5–6. It says, "Punishing the children for the sin of the parents to the third and fourth generation of those who hate me, but showing love to a thousand generations of those who love me and keep my commandments." Contrary to some interpretations, this scripture is not teaching that God punishes innocent children for the mistakes of their parents. It also doesn't mean that you are doomed to repeat the same mistakes your parents made. And finally, it doesn't mean it's an unavoidable curse. For these reasons, this scripture must be harmonized with Ezekiel 18:20, which says, "The person who sins is the one who will die. The child will not be punished for the parent's sins, and the parent will not be punished for the child's sins" (NLT). However, there are natural consequences and spiritual patterns that often affect future generations, especially in homes where sin is not repented of and God is rejected. The phrase "of those who hate me" refers to those who continue in rebellion similar to their parents'. Conversely, the phrase "those who love me and keep my commandments" refers to those who are destined to break the cycle and set their family on a new path.

Notice that if these patterns are not broken, they can be passed down to the third and fourth generations. However, Moses employed hyperbole—a thousand generations—to illustrate the extent to which God desires to extend mercy to those who are determined to pass down new legacies.

Recognizing these generational soul chains in our lives is not about blaming your family of origin. It's about being determined to break the chains and start new, godly patterns to pass down to the next generation. When you first identify these patterns that have been passed down to you, you can position yourself to choose a different legacy for you and your family. When I got married in 2015, I was determined to break the chain of divorce in my family. I was determined to model for my children what a godly marriage looks like, so that, by God's grace, they will be able to model the same in their homes one day. Thankfully, God doesn't hold us responsible for the sins of our parents. Nor does

He give us a pass to continue these cycles simply because that's what we've been exposed to.

Soul Chain 4: Sexual Sin Soul Chains

I've heard it said, "Overcoming the habit of sexual sin is like riding a bike; you have to be prepared to fail, but you must persist."[3] This is undoubtedly the most common soul chain that people (primarily men) reach out to our ministry for help to overcome. These soul chains are compulsive patterns of lust, fantasy, or immoral behavior that distort God's design for intimacy and leave a person trapped in secrecy, shame, and false fulfillment.

The Enemy is having a field day with this type of soul chain because we live in a very sexualized culture. We can't even be on social media for five minutes without being bombarded by some sort of image or reel that is designed to tempt us to lust.

These soul chains, like all others, thrive on deception, convincing people that their sexual desires cannot be mastered or will never be fully met. Sadly, there are many different types of sexual sin soul chains.

- **Pornography addiction.** This is one of the most common types. It manifests when a person consumes explicit content that fuels their lust, distorts healthy intimacy, and creates unrealistic expectations, particularly within a marriage. Pornography can cause a spouse to feel as if they are competing against professional actors (or actresses), creating a sense of being undesirable in their spouse's eyes. Pornography trains the brain (using the same dopamine hit process we discussed earlier) to become aroused only when the person experiences something new, which inevitably can hinder natural arousal within marriage. This addiction is extremely dangerous because the images are on constant repeat in the mind, making it seem impossible to escape. It can also create insecurity on both the male and female sides. Several years ago, a young Christian man who was engaged reached out to our ministry. He was struggling with a porn addiction, which created an insecurity within him. He was petrified that he would not be able to please his future wife sexually because he was not built like the male porn actors he saw on the screen, and he almost called off the wedding because of it. This is how damaging and controlling a soul chain of this type can be.

- **Masturbation and lustful fantasies.** This is one that many people engage in because our culture promotes it as a safe way to explore one's sexuality. After all, you're not hurting anyone if you're doing it to yourself. But this is a deception from the Enemy, because what he doesn't want people to know is that, if not broken, this soul chain can follow them into their marriage and become the crutch they lean on when their sexual needs aren't being met. Instead of working with their spouse to ensure their needs are met, they can be tempted to use this as a backup plan to "take matters into their own hands."
- **Premarital sex.** This is when a person engages in any kind of sexual activity outside of God's design for marriage, whether penetrative or nonpenetrative. It ultimately leads to negative emotional and spiritual consequences. Premarital sex promises short-term pleasures while always hiding the long-term consequences. This is accepted, encouraged, and even celebrated in our culture today.
- **Adultery and infidelity.** This involves betraying marital vows through either emotional or physical unfaithfulness. It ultimately damages trust and breaks the covenant relationship of marriage. And as it's been said, "Trust is earned in drops but lost in buckets."
- **Homosexual behavior.** Satan's got so many people in bondage

with this one—both inside and outside the Church. His strategy is to normalize sin so that people no longer feel a sense of embarrassment or guilt. Homosexuality is primarily seen as an alternative lifestyle rather than an abomination to God.

- **Sexual exploitation and prostitution.** Those actively involved in the pornography industry are in bondage to this soul chain and don't even realize it. They often enter the industry due to another soul chain discussed later: low self-esteem.
- **Serial relationships and hookup culture.** The Enemy's strategy is to remove the sanctity of sex by minimizing it. Enter the hookup culture, where individuals move from one sexual partner to another, using relationships for personal gratification without commitment.
- **Fantasy and erotic literature.** Some get caught up in lustful patterns through books, media, or entertainment that promote sexual immorality and distort God's view of purity.
- **Covert sexual sin.** This involves engaging in seemingly "harmless" behaviors like inappropriate flirting, sexting, or emotional affairs that lead to deeper compromise.
- **Sexual identity confusion.** Some struggle with gender identity or sexual orientation in ways that conflict with biblical truth and God's design.

Now that we understand the different types of sexual sin soul chains, here are several ways we can begin to identify them in our lives.

- You struggle with recurring sexual temptation or behaviors that feel impossible to stop.
- You feel shame and harbor secrecy, hiding your struggles from others.
- You have justified or minimized certain sexual sins, convincing yourself they are not serious.

- You have felt distant from God or struggled spiritually because of unconfessed sin in this area.
- You have secret chats with someone who is not your spouse and you find yourself becoming either physically or emotionally attached to them.
- You use sexual behavior as a way to cope with stress, loneliness, or emotional pain.
- You experience guilt or conviction after engaging in sexual sin but return to it anyway.
- You feel powerless against specific desires or habits, despite wanting to change.
- You have damaged relationships due to sexual sin, such as infidelity, secrecy, or broken trust.
- You have allowed sexual temptation to take priority over your spiritual growth and relationship with God.

Regardless of how hopeless you may feel when battling sexual soul chains, even these are not too powerful that Jesus can't break them. They also must bow before the transformative power of the Holy Spirit. We will explore this in more detail in the Process section.

Soul Chain 5: Relational Soul Chains

Relational soul chains are some of the most potent ways in which many believers continue to remain bound. Instead of reflecting God's intent and desire for healthy relationships, relational soul chains twist a person's expectations, tempt them to go beyond healthy boundaries, and lead to interactions that drain them spiritually and emotionally. We need to be aware of several different types of relational soul chains. The first is *codependency*. This is when we find our identity or worth in another person's approval, mood, or needs. In other words, we feel good about ourselves when that person approves of us. But our identity and stability shift when we don't get that approval. We get caught up in a vicious cycle of people-pleasing. Our primary responsibility is meeting their needs, even if that compromises our values and standards. If we see a flaw in our partner, we feel responsible for fixing it. We feel powerless to refuse their requests, even if they are unreasonable. We feel terrified of being alone.

Another common one is *fear of abandonment*. This is when we begin to see patterns in our relationships where we decide to stay with someone even though the relationship is toxic, because we're afraid they will abandon us. So we cling to them even more or look for ways to control the person or relationship. We may even sabotage the relationship because if the relationship ends, it won't be a result of being abandoned. We can just say that the relationship didn't work out.

A third type of relational soul chain is *isolation*. This is when we avoid meaningful relationships out of fear of being hurt. We fear being truly vulnerable in the relationship, so we protect ourselves from experiencing pain by isolating ourselves, not realizing this leads to a deeper level of loneliness and spiritual drift.

Sadly, these types of soul chains don't just impact our connections with others; they often leave a deep imprint on how we perceive ourselves. They can condition us to believe things about our worth, our identity, and our value to God. We can begin to accept the lies that take root, the ones that say, "I'm not enough," or "I'm only valuable if I perform." They can impact our identity, which is why we will end this chapter discussing these types of soul chains.

Soul Chain 6: Psychological Soul Chains

Some of the most dangerous and paralyzing soul chains are the ones that are the quietest. These are the ones that shape how we see ourselves.

Psychological soul chains are the scripts we rehearse in our minds about who we really are, what we're worth, and whether we're truly loved and accepted. These demonic scripts affect how we relate to others, and they even impact our calling. Let's expose several psychologically based lies that keep so many stuck.

Inferiority

Up first is the soul chain of *inferiority*. At its core, this soul chain says, "I'm not good enough." When we consistently compare ourselves to others and feel as though we come up short, this can be a sign that inferiority has taken root in our lives.

We become convinced that we're too weak, broken, unqualified, ill-prepared, or inadequate to be used by God. The whispers solidify the lie that others are more gifted, spiritual, and qualified than we are. As a result, this mindset imprisons us, keeping us from exercising the confidence to step into our calling because we are paralyzed by fear and doubt.

Moses is the poster child for this type of soul chain. (Sorry, Moses.) When God called Moses at the burning bush to lead the Israelites out of Egyptian bondage, Moses didn't respond with confidence. He responded with insecurity. He devised every excuse in the book to turn down the assignment. However, notice in the following story that each time Moses tried to give an excuse, God had an answer. And His answer wasn't to build up Moses's self-confidence but to give Moses more confidence in Him.

Excuse 1: "Who am I?"

Moses's first excuse is found in Exodus 3:11, "Who am I to appear before Pharaoh? Who am I to lead the people of Israel out of Egypt?" (NLT).

Notice God's response to him in verse 12. "I will be with you." God essentially said, "Moses, what I'm calling you to is much bigger than you. It's about who I am, and since I'll be with you, it's not about who you are. It's about who I am through you." This is an excellent reminder for us when we feel inferior or suffer from impostor syndrome. Moses figured, "Well, that obviously didn't work. Let me come up with a different excuse."

Excuse 2: "This probably won't work!"

So next he said, "What if they won't believe me or listen to me? What if they say, 'The LORD never appeared to you'?" (4:1 NLT).

At his core, Moses was dealing with a fear of failure. What if this doesn't work? So God gave Moses three miraculous signs: the staff turning into a snake, the leprous hand being healed, and water turning to blood.

God confirmed His power through Moses with these miraculous signs. This is something we must always keep in mind when we are called to a particular task. It's not about our power but the power of God working through us. Well, Moses was not done. He had another excuse up his sleeve!

Excuse 3: "I'm not a good speaker."

Intent on convincing God he was not the right man for the job, Moses launched his third excuse in verse 10, saying, "O Lord, I'm not very good with words. . . . I get tongue-tied, and my words get tangled" (NLT).

Moses assumed that God had made a mistake in choosing him because clearly, God didn't know that Moses had a speaking problem, right?

Notice God's response. "Who makes a person's mouth? . . . Is it not I, the LORD? Now go! I will be with you as you speak, and I will instruct you in what to say" (verses 11–12 NLT).

God reminded Moses that whatever limitations he felt he had were no surprise to God. In fact, God is the One who designed Moses, which means He knew about the speaking problem before He called him.

Finally, Moses realized that none of his excuses would suffice, and the truth was revealed.

Excuse 4: "Please send someone else!"

"Lord, please! Send anyone else" (verse 13). I want you to notice that God didn't become angry at any of the other excuses Moses gave. This gives us insight into the heart of God. He understands that we will struggle with inferiority and inadequacy. And when we do, He will meet us where we are. What angered God was Moses's unwillingness to fulfill the assignment He had given him.

Notice His response in verses 14–15: "What about your brother, Aaron? I will help both of you speak" (my paraphrase). Even when Moses tried to retreat completely, God met him with patience and provision, ensuring he wasn't alone in the task.

We can learn a lot from this story. Whenever Moses pointed to his inadequacy, God pointed right back to His sufficiency. Every excuse Moses made was rooted in self-focus. Every answer God gave was rooted in God-focus.

This story leads us to a very profound truth: God is more concerned with our availability than our ability.

Performance

Another psychological soul chain that often flies well under the radar is the soul chain of *performance.* It essentially says, "I am what I do. My worth is tied to my success, productivity, or spiritual performance." It is the false belief that your value comes from how much you achieve, how well you perform, and how others perceive your accomplishments.

This is very different from legalism. Legalism occurs when we feel we need to perform to earn God's approval. It is when we need to perform to feel internal approval or approval by others. This is a common phenomenon in both the corporate world and ministry. A person's identity may become attached to what they do. When they perform well or up to their own standards, they feel better about themselves. When they perform below their expectations, they feel horrible because their identity is tied to their performance.

Not many people know this, but in 2023, I was on the verge of giving up on YouTube. My team and I were working tirelessly to produce what we thought were great videos, but they simply weren't reaching the audience we had hoped for. Every Tuesday, I would publish a video and closely monitor its performance. If I saw the video performing well, I was overcome with a sense of pride, excitement, and joy. But when the video underperformed, I was highly discouraged and felt like a failure. Because we were in a stretch where most of the videos were underperforming, my self-worth plummeted because it was tied to video performance. I sank into a place of deep discouragement and stayed there for months. It took God using my wife to speak into my life to pull me out of the funk I was in. She had to remind me that my worth was bigger than whether YouTube's algorithm showed my video to millions of people. She reminded me to release that burden to God and to celebrate however many people God allowed to see my videos. And from that moment, I felt like I had broken through! Do I still wrestle with discouragement at times? Yes. But I'm not overwhelmed or dominated by it the way I was in 2023.

Before we proceed, is there something other than Christ that you are attaching your identity to? Do you find your self-esteem, joy, and happiness rising and falling with your performance?

My friend Taylor Alesia experienced freedom from the soul chain of performance. Taylor had the kind of online fame most teenagers can only dream of. She had millions of followers. Constant attention. Money was pouring in. She was well known all over the internet for her beauty and the life she portrayed on social media. But behind the camera, Taylor was deeply broken.

As a teenager, she battled intense feelings of insecurity and low self-worth. Like so many young girls, she believed the demonic lie that her value was tied to how attractive others thought she was. So she started posting provocative pictures of herself online. The more attention she garnered from these pictures, the more it became like a drug. It grew addictive, and she wanted more and more. And to make matters worse, she was making tons of money. However, as a result of the soul chain of low self-worth and people-pleasing, she entered into several toxic relationships, taking her further away from a relationship with Christ.

She craved validation, and every like, comment, and share became a dopamine hit of temporary approval. As she got older, she turned to platforms similar to OnlyFans, thinking it would give her even more control, financial independence, and freedom. And it did, for a while—on the surface at least. Over time, she began to feel more like a product than a person. The freedom she thought she had found quickly turned into a form of bondage.

But amid all of this, God was working behind the scenes in her life. She began to question, "Why am I still so anxious? Why do I still feel empty when I have everything the world says I should want?" These unanswered questions led her to seek something of even greater value. That's when she encountered Jesus Christ for the first time.

As she learned the truth of God's Word, she realized she didn't need to earn love from others or God. She didn't need to post another picture to be validated. She didn't need to keep performing to be accepted. She found her purpose and value in Christ apart from social media.

One day, she boldly decided to walk away from it all. She deleted all the provocative pictures she had posted of herself online and completely stepped out of the influencer lifestyle. She started a new online profile called The Bible Chick, where she teaches the Bible, shares her story, and reminds others that true freedom comes from knowing who you are in Christ. Today she's a wife and mother and is thriving in ministry.

This was not an overnight transformation. Even after leaving the lifestyle, it took time and intentionality to break away completely.

Victim mentality

Another type of psychological soul chain is a *victim mentality.* This is when someone's identity is attached to their pain or trauma, and they are convinced that nothing will ever get better for them because they are no greater than their pain. They feel powerless, defeated, and permanently stuck in the narrative of what others did to them or what life has taken from them. If you recall, this was Cameron's soul chain. Here are several things that someone struggling with this soul chain may consistently say to others or themselves:

- Why does this always happen to me?
- Nothing ever works out in my favor.
- People always leave me or let me down.
- I've been through too much to ever truly heal.
- No one really understands what I've been through.
- God must love others more than He loves me.
- Even when I try, it never makes a difference.
- There's no point in hoping anymore; it just leads to disappointment.
- I'll never get past what happened to me.
- Everyone else has it easier.
- I can't trust anyone; people always hurt me.
- I'm always the one who gets overlooked or left out.
- My life is ruined because of what they did to me.
- I just wasn't meant to be happy or whole.

Constantly rehearsing these scripts, either to others or to themself, only promises to keep a person bound in depression and hopelessness.

Not to mention, it goes directly against what the Bible says about them (more on this in a later chapter).

Low self-worth

Another psychological soul chain is *low self-worth*. This is when a person has a distorted view of themself rooted in shame, rejection, or comparison, leading them to feel inadequate, unlovable, or undeserving of God's love and purpose.

This soul chain can develop from negative words spoken over a person over a period of time, past trauma, or a lack of affirmation in childhood or significant relationships. Instead of seeing themself as God sees them, and others, too, for that matter, they believe the demonic lie that they are just not good enough.

Here are a few practical ways to identify the soul chain of low self-worth in our lives:

- You constantly compare yourself to others and feel like you never measure up.
- You struggle to accept compliments or believe positive things about yourself.
- You often feel invisible, overlooked, or as though your presence doesn't matter.
- You engage in self-sabotage, avoiding opportunities because of the fear of failure.
- You base your worth on external validation—such as achievements, appearance, or approval from others.
- You stay in unhealthy relationships because you don't believe you deserve better.
- You feel unworthy of God's love and struggle to believe He has a purpose for you.
- Your harsh inner critic constantly reminds you of your flaws and past mistakes.

Leah and Rachel's story in Genesis 29–30 illustrates how low self-worth can take root through comparison, rejection, and misplaced identity. Leah grew up in the shadow of her younger sister, Rachel, who was described as "beautiful of form and appearance" (Genesis 29:17 NKJV), while Leah was simply noted as having "weak eyes." Wow, the Bible doesn't hold back, does it? How would you feel if people described you as having "weak eyes"? Even from the beginning, Leah's identity was marked by comparison, and she likely felt she was never enough. Her sister was the beautiful one, and she was average-looking at best.

Her father, Laban, even had to trick Jacob into marrying her instead of her sister, Rachel, because she (Leah) was the firstborn daughter. This resulted in Leah being in a loveless marriage, knowing all along that her husband, Jacob, really loved Rachel (the pretty one) and had only married Leah out of obligation. Imagine what this must have done to her self-worth. Because she was unloved, she believed that she could win Jacob's affection by bearing him children. Each time she gave birth to a son, she named the son in a way that revealed her desperate need for validation.

- **Reuben:** "It is because the Lord has seen my misery. *Surely my husband will love me now*" (Genesis 29:32).
- **Simeon:** "Because the Lord heard that *I am not loved*, he gave me this one too" (verse 33).
- **Levi:** "Now at last *my husband will become attached to me*" (verse 34).

Her entire identity was not centered on how God saw her but rather on her performance and how she perceived her husband saw her. Her soul chain of low self-worth was primarily rooted in rejection.

Her sister, Rachel, also struggled with low self-worth. Because she was unable to conceive, she constantly compared herself to her sister and felt unworthy. In that culture, a woman was considered cursed if she was unable to bear children. Rachel even cried out in despair in Genesis 30:1, "Give me children, or I'll die!" Her struggle reveals how even those who seem to "have it all going on" can battle feelings of low self-worth on the inside when their identity is tied to external validation.

The point of this story is that both women struggled with low self-worth. Leah's was rooted in rejection, while Rachel's was rooted in comparison.

Many years ago, when I was single, I dated a young lady whom I thought was stunningly beautiful. As a matter of fact, everyone thought she was. Everyone, that is, except her. The more I got to know her, the more I saw how she focused on everything she saw that was wrong with herself. She picked herself apart and had created a mental laundry list of physical defects, leading her to conclude that she was unattractive. One day it was her nose. The next it was her knees. Then it was the bags under her eyes.

And the list went on and on. She couldn't see what others saw and what God saw in her. As I dug deeper, I found that most of her insecurities were formed through someone saying these things about her at some point in her past. She believed what others saw in her rather than what God saw in her. This is precisely what we talked about in the previous chapter: Soul chains originate from lies we believe.

Perfectionism

The final type of psychological soul chain we will explore is *perfectionism*. This soul chain convinces a person that they must always be perfect to be accepted, loved, or valued. Instead of embracing grace and progress, perfectionism drives a person to constantly strive, avoid failure at all costs, and fear disappointing others or God.

Perfectionism often leads to exhaustion, anxiety, and frustration because no one can truly live up to the unrealistic standards it demands. It traps a person in cycles of self-criticism, people-pleasing, and fear of failure, making it difficult for them to experience the joy and freedom God intends.

This can manifest itself in at least four ways. First, *a fear of failure can overcome us.* We discussed this earlier in the soul chain of fear. This is when we are convinced that making a mistake means we are inadequate or unworthy. It often leads us to avoid taking significant risks or opportunities altogether because the thought of failing is a blow to our ego, confidence, and self-worth. Someone struggling with this soul chain might say, "If I mess up, I will let everyone down." Instead of seeing failure as a chance to learn and grow, they view it as undeniable proof that they are not good enough, leading to paralysis and missed growth opportunities.

Another way perfectionism manifests itself is through *a constant need for approval from others.* Individuals with a soul chain of perfectionism often feel that their worth is determined by how others perceive them. They strive to be perfect because, in their minds, this is the only way in which people will truly respect or accept them. This mindset leads to a constant need for validation from others to feel worthy. Criticism or disapproval feels devastating because it reinforces the belief that they are not good enough. Instead of resting in God's approval, they rely on human affirmation to feel secure, which creates a cycle of anxiety and self-doubt.

Perfectionism also manifests itself through *extremely harsh self-criticism.* A person trapped in perfectionism often hold themself to impossible standards, believing that anything less than flawless performance is failure. They may constantly think, "I'll never be good enough," reinforcing feelings of inadequacy. This mindset leads them to set unrealistic expectations for themselves, and when they inevitably fall short, they feel like a failure. Even when they achieve some level of success, they fail to celebrate the progress, and it's quickly dismissed and replaced with a sense of "it's still not good enough." This cycle of relentless self-judgment robs them of joy and keeps them from embracing God's grace.

Ultimately, perfectionism *influences our perspective on our relationship with God*. Spiritual perfectionism is the belief that our relationship with God is based on perfect obedience rather than grace (similar to legalism). A person struggling with this soul chain may constantly think, "God won't love me unless I get everything right." Regardless, this mindset leads to an exhausting cycle of seeking God's approval through religious performance (legalism) rather than resting in His love. We struggle to truly accept God's grace and often feel distant from God whenever we fall short. Instead of viewing mistakes as opportunities for growth, we see them as proof of our unworthiness, making it difficult for us to experience the freedom and peace that God offers.

Perfectionism has been a lifelong struggle for both me and my wife. It has affected every area of my life. One specific area involves competing in sports. Recently I was competing in a pickleball tournament, and my wife and our kids (seven and eight years old at the time) came to support me. My teammate and I won the first few games and I was feeling good. But when we went to the playoffs, I made several mistakes that cost our team the game. And toward the end of the game, I got so angry that I violently threw my pickleball paddle on the ground. It made such a loud sound that it drew the attention of other players on the courts beside me. But what was most embarrassing is that I did this right in front of my wife and kids. I did not set a good example that day of what it means to lose gracefully. I allowed my perfectionism to get the best of me, and I still regret that moment to this day.

Conclusion

I know that was bumpy, trust me. If I'm being honest, it was difficult for me to write, because it took me places I would have preferred not to go. Maybe you're feeling the same way. Perhaps this chapter challenged you to forgive someone. You've been holding on to the bitterness, and God is saying to let it go. Maybe you've realized that you have a low self-image, which is contributing to the struggles in your relationships. Maybe you are dominated by fear and anxiety, and you struggle to experience the peace and joy God intends. Maybe you're working with some sort of addiction. Or, finally, maybe this chapter encouraged you to explore some things that happened in your family of origin during your childhood that you would rather have left alone. I know this is not easy, but it's the necessary work you must do to experience the freedom both you and God want. I'm with you every step of this journey, and I trust God with you, knowing that there is freedom on the other side. Let's get there together.

REFLECTION QUESTIONS

1. Which category of soul chain (spiritual, emotional, generational, sexual, relational, or psychological) most resonates with your current struggles? Why?

2. Which *specific* soul chain described in this chapter best reflects what you're currently facing or have faced in the past?

3. Are there any patterns or behaviors in your life that seem tied to more than one type of soul chain?

4. Are there any areas where your relationships consistently become strained, distant, or dysfunctional due to repeated patterns?

5. Which psychologically based soul chain (e.g., low self-worth, performance, rejection) do you most relate to, and how has it shaped the way you see yourself?

6. Are there any generational patterns or family dynamics that seem to repeat themselves in your thoughts, behavior, or relationships?

7. Do you notice soul chains in your life that you've normalized or dismissed simply because they've been part of your story for so long?

CHAPTER 3

WHEN CHAINS SHAPE YOUR LIFE

In 2002, while I was in seminary, I got engaged. My fiancée and I were six months away from tying the knot. We had an engagement party in Dallas, and all of my family came down from Pittsburgh to celebrate us. We had another party in Pittsburgh, where her family traveled to meet mine. I bought the ring. She bought the dress. The down payment for the reception hall was paid. Honeymoon plans were secured. Then, through a series of events that will remain private, that relationship ended, leaving us both in heartbreak hotel. Shortly after that, I got seriously involved with another young lady whom I thought I would marry. But that relationship ended as well.

About a year later, in 2004, I graduated from Dallas Theological Seminary with a master of theology, holding high hopes for a full-time ministry career. But things didn't work out quite the way I had planned. For the next ten years, I went from one relationship to the next, as I shared earlier. However, what I didn't share was that while all this was happening, I applied to every open full-time ministry position I could find. Whether it was for a teaching pastor, youth pastor, or worship pastor, I applied for the position. To my utter shock and dismay, I got rejected from every single one. So I started teaching high school math in 2006 to make ends meet. I figured I would only have to do this for a year or two since I had aspirations to be in full-time ministry. I ended up teaching high school for eleven years. As much as I thought I was ready to be on staff at a megachurch as a teaching pastor, preaching and teaching in front of thousands, I wasn't. Why? My dating relationships were a distraction. My soul chain of fear of commitment, which I developed in childhood, combined with my soul chain of self-pleasure, kept me in a perpetual state of frustration, conviction, and discouragement. These ultimately hindered me from walking in my divine purpose for over ten years.

This is just one of the ways failing to gain victory over your soul chain can impact your life, which in turn affects the impact you have on other people's lives. And that's significant.

We've examined soul chains in detail, including their formation, various types, and how to recognize them in our lives. But now we must address a sobering question: What happens if we don't deal with them? What will it actually cost us if we remain tied to them? The purpose of this chapter isn't to evoke guilt or fear but to provide clarity. Soul chains are not neutral. If left unchecked, they grow. They deepen. We need to know what they are costing us so we can engage in a serious battle and achieve victory.

Soul chains are like cracks in a home's foundation. At first, they seem small, manageable. But over time, they get bigger and bigger, and the next thing we know, we have a serious problem with our foundation that cannot go unaddressed. However, by that point, the damage has already been done. This is how soul chains work. We don't want things to reach this point.

Before we discuss the *process* for breaking through in the next chapter, we need to pause and take an honest look at what's at stake if we don't break free. What have your soul chains already cost you? A better question is, What might they continue to steal if left unchallenged?

This chapter will examine how soul chains impact nearly every aspect of our lives, including our identity, relationships with others, intimacy with God, emotional well-being, and, unfortunately, even our sense of purpose. I pray that you aren't discouraged but instead are reminded that freedom is worth fighting for and is waiting for you on the other side. Let's dive in!

Soul Chains Sabotage Relationships

The sad reality concerning soul chains is that they don't just affect us; they impact those closest to us. My wife and I have a great marriage, but it's not perfect. Both of us have unresolved issues from our childhood that have negatively impacted our marriage.

I'll never forget one evening when I was sitting on the couch playing chess on my iPad (as I often do), and my wife came into the room and said, "Babe, something needs to change! You are addicted to screens! You don't realize how much screens preoccupy you and take you away from the family. You're here, but you're not present. The kids need you to be present. I need you to be present, but instead, these screens have your attention. You have a unique opportunity to positively impact these kids' lives through your presence, words, and influence. But you're always sitting in front of a screen!"

I was utterly taken aback, and to be honest, I was also confused and offended. In my mind, I was doing so much, but apparently it wasn't enough. So I lashed back, "When am I supposed to have downtime? Since you don't work outside the home, you get to have time to yourself throughout the day to do what you want to do and rest if you want. When do I get that time?"

I figured that after working hard all day, being the sole provider for our home, actively participating in our kids' sporting events, and helping out around the house here and there, I was doing more than enough. Certainly I was doing more than other dads and husbands, right? It got to a point where screens became my escape. Whether it was watching YouTube videos or sporting events, responding to my team members, or playing chess, I was consumed by screens. I didn't even realize the negative impact it was having on my family. Sometimes I would even completely detach from the family and go upstairs to watch TV by myself, leaving my wife and our two children downstairs when I should have been more present with them.

But it wasn't just about screens; the issue went much deeper than that. Growing up without a father in the home created a void within me that I didn't even fully realize until much later in life. It was like layers of onions being peeled back one by one. The more I lived, the more I realized how much not having an active father in the home impacted me, and this was a perfect example. Since I didn't have my father at home, I felt lost and confused about how to spend quality time with my children beyond what I saw growing up. So I did what I knew to do: work hard, provide for my family, be a faithful husband, help out with sports, and assist around the house here and there. But my wife was bleeding out and desperate for more of my presence in the home. My soul chain of a father wound was hurting our family, and it needed to be addressed. Over time, we had to set strict boundaries for screen usage to ensure that during certain times of the evening, I was fully present to maximize the limited time we have with our children.

My wife, Jennifer, has her own issues from her childhood that were negatively impacting our marriage. She was born in Nigeria, and at the time of her birth, things were getting bad there. So her family moved to the States when she was five years old. However, not everyone was able to come at the same time. She, her sister, and her mother immigrated, while her father and her two brothers stayed back in Nigeria. They remained a separated family for several years until her father and brothers could safely make their way to the States. During this time, her mother was forced to be the sole provider for their family. She worked extra jobs to ensure her family was well taken care of. Even after Jennifer's father moved to the States, he wasn't able to secure solid employment like he had back home in Nigeria.

As a result, my wife came into our marriage struggling to relinquish control. She had grown up in a home where her mother was the primary provider. This caused her to believe that she could not depend on a man to take care of her and that she always needed to have a plan B. This created significant issues in our home, particularly when our children were young. She had a lucrative career at a major Fortune 500 company. But that career took her further and further away from our family. She secretly struggled with mommy guilt because she knew she wasn't present enough for our kids, who were one and two years old at the time. Kids were picked up late from day care. Meals were thrown together at the last minute. Our intimacy was impacted due to her fatigue. Our marriage was still relatively new, and our ministry was growing exponentially. I needed more support. But in her mind, she had to work "just in case something happens to her husband." She struggled to trust me and God to truly provide for her.

My wife was dealing with several soul chains. Although she was married to a hardworking, faithful, trustworthy man (that would be me), that inner voice told her, "What if something happens to him? To feel safe and secure, I need to be in control at all times and cannot trust others. If I don't, I'll just be disappointed, or worse, not provided for." Another soul chain was a performance identity. She derived more of her identity from being a high-income earner at a Fortune 500 company than from embracing her identity as a wife and mother.

Both my wife and I brought soul chains into our marriage that we didn't even realize were there, and they caused damage in the earliest stages of our marriage and family.

As you can see, soul chains can harm our earthly relationships. However, the deepest damage occurs in our relationship with God. Some soul chains cause us to feel too dirty to pray. Some cause us to keep

God at arm's length, afraid of what He might ask of us. Others cause us to see God in a way that is contrary to His character. Ultimately, they hinder our ability to experience intimacy with God.

Soul Chains Hinder Spiritual Growth and Intimacy with God

A young lady shared this story with our ministry. As far back as she can recall, Bri had always felt different, but she could never explain exactly why. By the time she was in middle school, she began noticing that she felt more emotionally drawn to girls than to boys, particularly in ways her peers didn't seem to. Initially, she brushed it off as just a phase. But as she entered high school, the feelings didn't go away. Instead, they intensified.

Bri grew up in church. Her parents were actively involved in ministry. She was known in church for her sweet spirit, beautiful singing voice, and heart for God. But privately, she carried a burden no one knew about. She had heard people at church talk about "those people," often with disgust or condemnation. She never heard them talk about their love for "those people" or that there was grace, only judgment. So Bri made a conscious decision: "I can never let this part of me be seen . . . ever."

She became an expert at leading a double life. On Sundays, she led worship and then cried herself to sleep on Monday. Again and again, she begged God to take the feelings away, but when He didn't, she assumed God was angry with her. Over time, her prayers became nonexistent. Her worship lost sincerity. She began to avoid studying the Bible because every verse she read seemed to highlight her unworthiness. She no longer felt like a daughter of God. She became angry at God for "making her this way" and not answering her prayers to remove the feelings.

She eventually drifted away from church altogether, not because she stopped believing in God, but because she believed the lie that God wanted nothing to do with her. So now her soul chain wasn't just same-sex attraction, it was compounded with other soul chains like anger, shame, isolation, and fear (more on this later).

Then the time came when she finally gave in and acted on her feelings in a same-sex relationship. She was afraid it was only a matter of time before she was exposed and everyone knew her secret. And most of all, she feared that no matter how hard she tried, she would never live up to God's standard. The soul chain within whispered, "You're too far gone. God cannot love you."

The irony of this story is that she distanced herself from the very God who had the power to heal her, not realizing that God wasn't looking for perfection; He was waiting for surrender.

Marcus never missed a Sunday. Or a Wednesday. Or a men's breakfast, a volunteer meeting, or a church workday. You get the point. He was the kind of guy who always showed up early, prepared and ready to serve. From the outside, he was a pillar in his church community. He was dependable, disciplined, and deeply committed. But on the inside, Marcus was exhausted.

Marcus grew up in a strict religious environment where obedience, service, rules, and visible acts of righteousness were used to measure spirituality. He was taught that emotions should be suppressed. Rest was discouraged, and grace was treated as a license for laziness. As time passed, Marcus began to associate God's love and approval with his performance. The more he did, the more God was pleased. If he slipped up and fell short, God was angry with him.

So he kept doing—more and more.

He read his Bible every day, but it felt more like something he did to check off a box and appease God rather than something focused on connecting with God. He prayed, but mostly to confess where he had failed. When asked how he was doing, he would respond with his typical answer: "Just staying busy and faithful." Behind that response, Marcus felt spiritually dry and wholly disconnected from God. He didn't know how to rest in God's love, only how to work for it.

As the years passed, he began to secretly resent the faith he had once loved. He grew weary of being at the church five days a week.

He didn't feel joy. He didn't feel peace. Instead, he felt pressure. His relationship with God had become transactional: "The more I do, the more I'll earn God's approval." But he spiraled into guilt whenever he fell short (skipping a devotional, missing his prayer time, not showing up to serve at church, etc.). This led him to try even harder the next time to make up for where he fell short and get back in good standing with God.

Marcus never realized that his legalism had become a soul chain. It was a mindset that convinced him God's love was conditional and that rest was a sign of weakness. He never saw God as a loving Father but rather as a harsh taskmaster who was demanding, distant, and constantly evaluating his every move.

Soul Chains Steal Purpose and Delay Destiny

I'm convinced that the most dangerous effect of a soul chain is the one we notice last: It slowly steals your sense of purpose and ultimately delays the destiny and calling God created you to walk in. We often assume that our soul chains are simply private battles we wage within our minds. But they never stay confined to one area of life. Instead, they are designed to completely hinder us from moving forward.

Soul chains cause us to live in a reactive mode, rather than a mission-driven one. We wake up thinking about how we will manage the battle rather than how we will advance the kingdom. We are focused more on survival than significance. It's hard to dream with God or say yes to new assignments when we're just trying to make it through the day.

We can become too distracted by our soul chain to hear God's voice clearly. We can feel so defeated that we don't even believe we have a calling.

Or we can feel so ashamed that we don't think we deserve to walk in it. We are convinced we must "get it together" before walking in our calling.

Samson: A Case Study on Toxic Relationships

The Bible contains a plethora of stories of people whose soul chains either delayed or threatened to derail their purpose. One of the most tragic stories is that of Samson in Judges 13–16.

When we think of Samson, we often think of the man with supernatural brute strength. He was a man chosen by God from birth, set apart by a Nazirite vow, which meant he had to abstain from wine, avoid contact with the dead, and never cut his hair. If he upheld this vow, God would continue to use him to lead Israel into victory over their enemies. However, like many men, Samson had a soul chain of lust and pride that ultimately led to the derailment of his calling. This was confirmed by a pattern of giving in to the wrong women. First, in Judges 14, he demanded a Philistine wife. "His father and mother objected. 'Isn't there even one woman in our tribe or among all the Israelites you could marry?' they asked. 'Why must you go to the pagan Philistines to find a wife?' But Samson told his father, 'Get her for me! She looks good to me'" (verse 3 NLT).

How many relationships today start with us saying the same thing Samson said? "I want her because she looks good to me."

Sometime later, his wife was taken away from him and given to his best man. Sheesh, you gotta feel for the guy! Well, instead of processing his pain in a healthy way, he had sex with a prostitute. "One day Samson went to the Philistine town of Gaza and spent the night with a prostitute" (Judges 16:1 NLT).

Shortly after this, he became involved with another Philistine woman named Delilah. She wanted to know the secret of Samson's supernatural strength. After he told her a series of playful lies, she became impatient and began to pout, putting more pressure on him until he shared the secret to his strength. She cut off his hair, and then we have one of the most sobering verses in the entire Bible. In verse 20 we read, "Then she cried out, 'Samson! The Philistines have come to capture you!' When he woke up, he thought, 'I will do as before and shake myself free.' But he didn't realize the LORD had left him" (NLT).

Samson's eyes were gouged out. He was bound, humiliated, and made to perform like a slave. The man who was called to lead Israel became a spectacle for its enemies. His pride and preoccupation with the wrong women caused him to live far beneath his potential. For many Christians, this is how the Enemy continues to trip us up. The soul chain of toxic relationships keeps us so preoccupied that we are unable to step into the calling God has for us.

King Saul: A Case Study in Insecurity

Israel's first king, Saul, illustrates how soul chains can derail or delay our purpose. He started well, but deep within, he wrestled with the soul chains of insecurity and fear of man.

Rather than resting in God's approval, Saul constantly sought affirmation from people. First Samuel 15 describes how he disobeyed God's command to execute the Amalekites and their king entirely. He made excuses, saying, "I was afraid of the people and did what they demanded" (verse 24 NLT). Saul's inability to deal with his internal soul chain led to his rejection as king. His disobedience not only delayed Israel's progress, it cost him his legacy. Not only that, it sabotaged meaningful relationships, including with David, his son Jonathan, and even his daughter Michal.

In addition to these biblical examples, there are countless modern-day examples of Christians who have failed to experience victory over soul chains, leading to either delaying their purpose or even being disqualified from it. Sadly, countless pastors have fallen into sexual sin, disqualifying them from ministry.

Speaking more generally, maybe it's a woman who feels too ashamed of her past to step out and mentor other women. Or perhaps it's a man who won't pursue ministry because he still battles with lust in secret. Or maybe it's the leader who fears failure so strongly that she overprepares, overthinks, and never moves forward.

The reality is that God is not waiting for our perfection; He's waiting for our surrender. But that quiet soul chain continues to whisper the lie that we must "clean ourselves up" before God can use us. It tells us, "When you finally break free from this, then and only then can you be obedient and be truly used by God." But the irony is that our obedience is what activates our freedom.

We need some good news right about now. The good news is that delay is not denial. Because of the soul chains I was battling for years, I questioned whether God would truly use me in a significant way. I finally broke free when I turned forty.

A year before that, in 2014, I met the most beautiful, amazing, kind, intelligent, caring, godly (should I go on? Yeah, I will), thoughtful, selfless woman a man could dream of meeting. It was Valentine's Day, and the church I was attending was having an eighties throwback party. I figured I wasn't doing anything, so I might as well attend. I'm so glad I did. The girl greeting people at the door had the most beautiful smile. We talked that night for about an hour, but it felt like only a few minutes because the conversation was so easy and natural. We began dating, and shortly after, she took a job in Washington, DC, against my wishes! So for the next year, we dated long-distance. On April 10, 2015, we got engaged, and we got married on my fortieth birthday, November 15, 2015. Everything went uphill from there.

A few months before we got married, on August 17, 2015, I published my first YouTube video on The BEAT. We started a math tutoring company together in 2017. And I was finally able to go full-time in ministry (a dream that took twenty years to realize) in 2020. And since then, God has blessed us with two beautiful children and an international ministry that reaches hundreds of millions of people worldwide. What's the point of my telling you all this? Where you are right now is *not* where you'll always be. God is not done writing your story. Your destiny may be delayed right now, but it's not denied. Delay does not mean disqualification.

Moses spent forty years on the back side of a desert before stepping into his calling. Perhaps he was dealing with guilt and feelings of failure after having committed murder in Egypt and being forced to run away. Yet he became Israel's greatest leader. Peter denied Jesus in His darkest hour but became the early church's primary leader. Paul was once a church persecutor, and God transformed him into a world-changing missionary. Don't let the devil convince you that your story is over. Don't let him put a period where God puts a comma. He's still writing your story, and that story is inviting you to surrender your soul chain to Him.

The Interconnectivity of Soul Chains

One of the most deceptive aspects of soul chains is that they rarely operate alone. The Enemy's ultimate goal is not simply to trap you in a single area but to gradually introduce more and more soul chains until your heart, mind, body, and entire life become thoroughly entangled. What begins as a simple foothold in one area can quickly multiply and spread like a spiritual infection that affects other dimensions of your life.

Unfortunately, Satan doesn't settle for partial bondage. His mission is to keep you bound emotionally, psychologically, relationally, sexually, and spiritually, all at once. These soul chains don't just coexist. They reinforce one another, creating a spiritual web that becomes increasingly difficult to escape the longer it remains unaddressed.

I experienced the interconnectedness of soul chains in my own life. The trauma of my parents' divorce when I was young and being raised in a single-parent home led me to never learn how to open up and truly express my emotions. Because we didn't have much, I developed a soul chain of a *poverty mindset*. I worried I wouldn't have enough to get by, which led to greed and selfishness. This led to the soul chain of a father wound—a natural chain that develops when there is no father present in the home. My fear of divorce led to a soul chain of *fear of commitment* and got me into unhealthy relationships. This led to an extended season of singleness, which in turn led to the soul chain of *self-pleasure*, which subsequently led to the soul chain of *anger* toward God and others. And if I'm being 100 percent transparent, I've struggled at times with being an *emotionally present* husband and father, as I shared earlier. What I want you to see is that these soul chains are interconnected.

Soul chains are nothing more than spiritual gateways. What starts as something seemingly small and manageable can become an entry point for multiple lies, behaviors, and belief systems that keep us trapped in deep bondage.

That's why Scripture warns us in Ephesians 4:27, "Do not give the devil a foothold." A foothold easily becomes a soul chain, and a soul chain easily becomes a system of bondage.

Conclusion

By now you may be feeling the weight of your own soul chains. Perhaps you've seen exactly how they have sabotaged your relationships, hindered your intimacy with God, delayed your purpose, or possibly even opened the door to other soul chains. Maybe for the first time, you're connecting the dots and realizing how much these invisible chains have held you back. But . . .

This is *not* where your story ends. It's where it begins. Are soul chains real? Yes. But so is the power of our God. God's power to break any soul chain is greater than anything you may face right now.

The same Jesus who died to save you died to set you free. He is neither surprised nor intimidated by your pain or your chain. He has seen this demonic pattern before and has set millions free from it. And guess what? You're next.

The good news is that no matter how many soul chains have formed, how they formed, how long they've been there, or how deeply they've impacted your life and others, it's never too late to walk in freedom. Your past doesn't define your future. The grip of sin, fear, addiction, legalism, shame, perfectionism, or any other soul chain is no match for the resurrection power of Christ that lives within you!

In the following chapters, we will finally focus on the process by which you can break through. We'll explore how to experience that freedom for yourself, renew your mind, confront lies, break patterns, and walk confidently in the person God created you to be. Are you ready to start the upward path? Let's do it together!

REFLECTION QUESTIONS

1. Which relationship in your life has been most affected by a soul chain (either yours or someone else's)? How has it shaped your interactions, communication, or ability to trust?

2. In what ways have you seen a soul chain hinder your intimacy with God, whether through shame, legalism, fear, or feelings of unworthiness?

3. Are there areas in your life where you feel delayed or disqualified from stepping into God's purpose? Could a soul chain be the reason?

4. Reflect on the stories of Samson and King Saul. Which of these examples do you relate to more, and why?

5. Has one soul chain in your life opened the door to others? If so, what are they, and how have they become intertwined?

6. After reading this chapter, what would you say has been the most significant cost of not addressing your soul chains sooner, and what would you want to reclaim?

PART 2

WALKING THROUGH THE PROCESS

CHAPTER 4

THE MIRROR MOMENT

I have a really good friend named Terry. He and I were born three weeks apart. In fact, our mothers were best friends who grew up across the street from each other and graduated from high school together. Our families were extremely close while we were growing up. Every year we would spend Christmas Eve together. We never missed a year. We both graduated from high school in 1993 and decided to attend Case Western Reserve University together, planning to be roommates. Since we were both in the engineering program, we had many of the same friends and were involved in numerous similar activities. We were roommates for five years, from our undergraduate studies to graduate school. We were the best of friends. That is, until 2002. Toward the end of graduate school, Terry met a wonderful young lady and instantly fell in love. They got married in 2001. At the time, I was engaged to be married the following year, so it was easy for me to celebrate with him. But when my engagement fell through in early 2002, it drove a wedge between us. He was married. I was single. He was enjoying the blessings of married life. I was still struggling (just being real).

As the years passed, he began having children, and I was still alone. I noticed that our relationship began to change. We were no longer able to talk about the same things we used to. We had less in common. Our lives were headed in two different directions. His career was taking off, and he was thriving and making lots of money, while I was a single seminary student, struggling and with no children. We tried for years to keep in touch, but as time passed, our relationship gradually fizzled out and became superficial at best. I was forced to ask myself, "How and why did this happen?" I had to take a serious look at myself to determine the root cause of our relationship breakdown. The Lord showed me that I was dealing with a serious soul chain of jealousy/comparison. It was so deeply entrenched that I found it difficult to talk to Terry or even be around him. Every time I did, I was reminded that he had something I coveted desperately. He had a wife. He had money. He had children. He had a beautiful home. He had it all, and I was stuck with what felt like nothing. It wasn't until I recognized the soul chain of jealousy had destroyed our relationship and confessed it to him that we were able to rebuild our relationship. Now, many years later, our relationship is strong. But this would not have happened if I hadn't been willing to take a look within myself and confess my soul chain of jealousy that the Enemy was using to destroy one of my closest friendships.

In the previous chapters, we examined the *problem* of soul chains. And you may feel as if these chains are nearly impossible to break. However, over the next few chapters, we are going to discuss the *process* by which these chains can be broken. The key principle I want you to embrace in this chapter is: You cannot break what you don't first recognize. I encourage you to do some introspection and take ownership of the chains that have been holding you back. Once you do that, we can begin the process of breaking through them.

Time for Self-Examination

Again and again, Scripture commands us to examine ourselves. Why? Our hearts tend to deceive us into thinking we are fine when in reality, we may still be operating under some form of dysfunction. David said it this way in Psalm 139:23–24: "Search me, God, and know my heart; test me and know my anxious thoughts. See if there is any offensive way in me, and lead me in the way everlasting."

Self-examination is necessary because often our soul chains feel normal. For example, suppose you were raised in an environment where you were constantly criticized. You may have developed a perfectionist mindset, assuming that your worth is directly tied to your performance. Still, you never connect that mindset to a soul chain of inadequacy.

Self-examination is also essential because we tend to minimize or excuse our beliefs and behaviors. We tend to downplay or dismiss our struggles with statements such as, "Well, that's just the way I am," or "It's not that bad," or "Everyone deals with this." These types of internal statements cause us to minimize the soul chain, inhibiting us from confronting it.

Self-examination is also critical because the Enemy's strategy is to blind us to our own struggles. He wants us to walk in ignorance. Second Corinthians 4:4 says, "The god of this age has blinded the minds of unbelievers, so that they cannot see the light of the gospel that displays the glory of Christ, who is the image of God."

While this verse speaks specifically to unbelievers, it also speaks to Satan's general strategy, which is to keep people walking in darkness. His job is to convince you that your soul chain is anything but a problem, knowing that if he is successful, you'll never see a need to take steps to break through.

How to Know If a Soul Chain Still Has Power over You

It's one thing to recognize a soul chain, but it's another to know if it still has power over us. We don't want to assume that it's no longer controlling us just because we are aware of it or have given it to God through prayer. So, to discern whether something is a soul chain for you, consider the following signs.

Sign 1: Repeated Patterns of Defeat

While "repeated" may be subjective, ask yourself, "Do I repeatedly experience failure in a particular area?" In other words, you may experience momentary victory, but you find yourself right back in defeat far too often. Perhaps you've tried everything to change, but nothing has gotten you the results you're looking for, and you feel stuck.

Sign 2: Resistance to the Truth

Another significant sign of a soul chain's presence is when we resist the truth. When we hear or read something that challenges us in a particular area related to the soul chain, we immediately become resistant to it rather than accepting it, because inwardly we know that what we have just heard or read is going to challenge us to make some changes we may not be ready to make just yet. Sadly, this is how I responded when my wife confronted me about my screen time. One of the most evident signs of an active soul chain is responding defensively when faced with the truth. This truth may come from Scripture, the inner witness of the Holy Spirit, or via wise counsel.

Brittany never saw herself as a social media addict. She ran a small online business and had one hundred thousand followers on her Instagram account. Each day, she would encourage people with faith-based reels and eagerly await their responses. Checking her phone consistently was necessary and "part of her ministry," she'd say.

But it became a bigger problem than she realized. She scrolled everywhere. Whether it was at a red light, a lunch date, or even during church when the sermon felt like it was dragging a bit, she was on her phone. Even when she was out with her mom, she was half listening while responding to DMs on her phone. Her friends and family began to notice that it was a problem. "Hey, Britt? When we hang out, it seems like you're distracted. It's tough to keep your attention."

"Sorry. I'm just multitasking," she'd say. Her mentor tried to bring this to her attention, but she brushed it off as normal behavior, saying, "Oh no, I'm totally fine. It's just the way I connect with people. I can stop anytime."

But beneath the surface, she was anxious when she couldn't check her phone. It was the first thing she reached for in the morning and the last thing she put down before bed. Her mood tanked when her reels didn't perform well. If someone criticized her content, it would ruin her entire day. She missed out on authentic, genuine connections with the people all around her because she was too committed to reaching people online.

When confronted with the truth, Brittany's response was always the same: "I'm just doing what God called me to do." But in reality, her soul was chained to something that promised influence but was stealing intimacy.

As we consider Brittany's story, ask yourself honestly, "How do I respond when confronted with truth? Do I receive it, or am I resistant to it?"

Sign 3: Emotional Echoes

Ask yourself this question: Are there situations, words, or even people that provoke an extreme internal or external response in me? I call these *emotional echoes.* They are reminders of unresolved wounds or soul chains that still carry influence. Just as a loud sound can bounce off the walls of a canyon long after the original noise has stopped, emotional echoes are old experiences that reverberate into our present. The experience may be long over, but the feelings linger and resurface when something similar triggers that same pain.

Going back to the story of my relationship with Terry, my day could have been going great, but if someone mentioned his name, I was instantly flooded with discouragement. That reaction wasn't random; it was an emotional echo of a wound that had yet to heal. It was a sure sign that that soul chain still had a hold on me.

Maybe for you someone brings up a person's name and your heart sinks. Sadness or bitterness wells up, and you're not sure why. That could be a soul chain of unforgiveness echoing in the background.

Perhaps someone asks you to take on something you didn't want to do, and you say yes—again. But later you regret it. That's not just about boundaries; it could be the soul chain of people-pleasing still whispering the lie that it's wrong to say no.

Maybe you reach out to someone, and they don't text you back right away. You start imagining the worst. You feel rejected, overlooked, perhaps even abandoned. That could be a soul chain of betrayal or insecurity still influencing how you interpret silence.

Or maybe someone asks you about your past, and you feel a wave of fear. You're tempted to lie or downplay what happened. That's not just discomfort—that could be shame still echoing in your soul. These emotional echoes don't just reveal pain—they point to areas where the Spirit is still longing to bring healing. And they show you where your mind may still need to be renewed.

Sign 4: Secrecy

When there are areas of your life you refuse to share with others and choose to handle in private, even though you know they continue to be destructive, this is a clear sign that a soul chain is present. For instance, a man constantly clears his browsing history. A woman is involved in a sexual relationship outside of marriage. A woman immediately puts her phone down when her husband enters the room because she doesn't want him to know she was on her phone . . . again.

If there's something in your life that you would never want others to know about, there's a good chance that it holds some level of power over you.

■

I know that may have been difficult to read, but if you identified with any of these signs, don't let that discourage you; let it motivate you. Be thankful that the Holy Spirit is shining light on an issue that demands your full attention. God doesn't reveal things to us to condemn us but to heal and restore us. Remember, "The Lord is close to the broken-hearted and saves those who are crushed in spirit" (Psalm 34:18).

Exposing the Source, Not Just the Symptoms

If you've ever had computer issues, dealing with them can be a frustrating experience. Whether your computer is running slowly, apps are crashing, or error messages are consistently appearing, these are symptoms of a larger problem. One way to address them is simply to reboot your computer. However, if those issues persist, it could indicate a more severe underlying issue, such as a virus. In this case, a reboot won't solve the problem. You need a tool that can conduct a thorough examination of your entire internal system and permanently eliminate the root-level threat.

Similarly, recognizing that a soul chain is present is a good start, but we must be willing to delve into it much more deeply. We must be careful not to just address the symptoms and overlook the root cause. As it's been said: Let's not put Band-Aids on bullet holes.

Let's explore some ways we can address the source of our chains.

Symptoms vs. Source: Emotional Soul Chains

Let's take the soul chain of anxiety. On the surface, the symptoms may resemble chronic worry, panic attacks, a fear of the unknown, playing the what-if game, or a constant need for control. But the real source of anxiety may be a fear of abandonment or rejection, having grown up in a chaotic home where life was uncertain and unstable, or a lack of trust in the sovereignty of God. These sources may convince you that you must be in control of every situation or things won't work out the way you desire. The source is what ultimately needs to be dealt with.

The soul chain of depression or hopelessness may manifest itself in a deep sense of sadness or despair, an overall feeling of numbness, or a loss of interest in things that once brought you joy. But the source may be unhealed grief, trauma, or feelings of unworthiness.

On the surface, a low sense of self-worth may show up as constant self-criticism or an unrelenting need to be perfect. It may manifest itself in constantly comparing yourself to others, leading to a general feeling of inadequacy. It may appear as settling for toxic, unequally yoked relationships or, sadly, even mistreatment. But you have to go deeper. The true source is that you grew up feeling unseen, unappreciated, or undervalued. Maybe some words were spoken to you by a parent, teacher, coach, or authority figure that you've been replaying subconsciously for years. Perhaps you've bought into the lie that you have to earn people's love and acceptance.

Let's take a look at anger. Externally, you struggle with a quick temper or "outbursts of anger." Maybe you harbor grudges and refuse to forgive others for past offenses. Maybe you're bitter because you feel God has been unfair to you. But the source may be something much more profound. Perhaps you've been deeply betrayed by someone you once trusted, leaving an open wound that never healed. Maybe you're convinced that God let your offender off cheap and didn't (or won't ever) avenge what was done to you, so you hold on to feelings of revenge and bitterness. Maybe you're still angry about something that happened to you in the past that you've buried deep inside.

Symptoms vs. Source: Habitual Sin Soul Chains

As we've discussed, habitual sin soul chains are some of the most common types of soul chains Christians deal with. However, we must understand that sin itself isn't the most significant problem; instead, it's the driving force behind the sinful behavior that needs to be addressed.

Simply trying to stop the behavior without addressing its root cause will inevitably lead to more frustration, as the behavior will continue to resurface in various forms. Let's do some soul work and get to the root of some of these habitual sins.

Take some of the most common ones: lust and pornography addiction. On the surface, lust may manifest as an everlasting struggle to control impure thoughts. Or perhaps it's a regular practice of masturbation or an addictive pattern of consuming pornography.

But what if these were driven by deeper, unmet emotional needs, which can lead a person to seek intimacy in the wrong places? Or perhaps they were exposed to it at a young age, and it became an ingrained habit. It could even be the result of an insecurity or lack of self-worth, such that when they watch pornography, they get a sense of acceptance and worth. The real issue may be connected to an extreme sense of loneliness or rejection.

Do you see how important it is to dig deeper to identify the underlying sources? If you address these underlying causes, I promise you'll start to see patterns of victory emerge in your life.

One soul chain that is often overlooked is gluttony, or overeating. If you can't say "amen," just say "ouch!" It may appear on the surface that you're constantly eating large portions of food that are primarily unhealthy for you. But the source may be that you're overeating due to stress, loneliness, grief, or sadness. Or perhaps you're using food as an escape or reward.

Finally, let's look at the soul chain of workaholism and perfectionism. The symptoms may be that you're always working, unable to rest, feeling guilty when you're not being "productive," or you define your self-worth by your accomplishments. However, the deeper issue is that you feel validated when you work. It gives your ego a boost. Or you fear failure, so you believe that if you work harder, you can avoid failure, which would be a hit to your ego. Perhaps your insatiable desire to work is tied to a need for more money because you're secretly afraid you won't have enough to meet your needs one day (poverty mindset). Or possibly you've bought into the lie that rest equals laziness. Finally, perhaps you're using work as a distraction from some emotional or spiritual emptiness or a relational issue you don't want to address, so you pour yourself into work rather than dealing with the real issue. Do you see how important it is to get to the true source of our chains?

Symptoms vs. Source: Relational Soul Chains

Relational soul chains are, unfortunately, quite common. These are consistent patterns of dysfunction in connecting with others. They could be in friendships, dating, marriage, family, or authority relationships. They create barriers to healthy, God-honoring connections, often leading to repeated cycles of pain, conflict, or isolation. Here are a few that I encourage you to address.

The first is codependency. As I mentioned in chapter 2, this is an unhealthy emotional reliance on other people from whom we derive our happiness, security, or sense of fulfillment. Essentially, our identity and happiness are often tied to another person, at the expense of our own well-being. The symptoms may include constantly sacrificing our own needs to keep someone else happy. Or we are obsessed with how others perceive us. We struggle to say no. We struggle to set healthy boundaries. However, the real source of this problem may be our deep-seated fear of rejection, which leads us to believe that by meeting the other person's needs and sacrificing our self, we can protect our self from ever being rejected. Or the deeper issue may be that we don't feel we have any worth outside of the relationship, so we pour everything into it.

Another type of relational soul chain previously discussed in chapter 2 is toxic and/or abusive relationships. On the surface, it appears as though we go in and out of unhealthy or controlling relationships. We struggle to leave a relationship even though we know it may be harmful. Or we feel stuck in a cycle of emotional, verbal, or even physical abuse. But the source may be our insecurity and inability to believe we deserve better. Or we fear being alone, so we settle for something unhealthy to avoid being alone.

One type of relational soul chain that resonates with me is the tendency to isolate and avoid deep, meaningful relationships. When I was single, I struggled mightily with this, and I had no idea why until much later in life. It may manifest as difficulty trusting people, even if they have never caused us harm. Alternatively, we can maintain shallow relationships to avoid vulnerability. Or we feel lonely yet unwilling to truly open up to others. However, these are mere symptoms. What are the sources? Maybe there is a fear of betrayal or rejection, so if we never allow ourselves to get close and vulnerable, we'll protect ourselves from experiencing the pain of betrayal. Or perhaps this is connected to unresolved pain from past relationships or friendships. We've been hurt before and never dealt with that hurt, so subconsciously we put up an emotional barrier designed to protect ourselves from ever experiencing that pain again. Finally, it could be a result of unresolved childhood issues.

Now, there are many other soul chains that we could address here, but I hope you understand the purpose of this section. It's about encouraging us to look beyond the symptoms to reach the source of our issues. If we don't address the source, our issues will continue to occur, leaving us feeling frustrated and hopeless.

Conclusion

I know it's not easy to peel back the layers of your past and look inward. Honestly, it's not fun at all. However, I commend you for doing the hard work and truly identifying the very thing(s) that have been holding you back for some time. Your soul chain(s) may be different than mine, but they all have a source. Staying on the surface and dealing with the symptoms will only keep you where you are. God wants you to be free, truly free. To do that, you must be willing to do the soul work required. I'm here cheering you on because, for the soul chains I acknowledged in my own life, I can celebrate that I have broken through! And if I can, I know by the power of God's Spirit, you can as well!

REFLECTION QUESTIONS

1. What's one area of your life that has felt "normal" for so long that you haven't considered it might be a soul chain?

2. Have you ever excused a destructive mindset or behavior with phrases like "that's just the way I am" or "everyone struggles with this"?

3. In what situations do you find yourself stuck in a repeated cycle of failure, frustration, or defeat, and what lies might be feeding that pattern?

4. When someone confronts you with truth through Scripture, a sermon, or a trusted friend, are there specific topics that trigger defensiveness or discomfort?

5. Can you identify any emotional echoes in your life that elicit an overreaction? What experience or internal belief could be driving that response?

6. Is there anything in your life that you work hard to hide from others—something you'd be embarrassed or ashamed for people to know?

7. For any struggle you're facing right now, have you been addressing the external symptoms, or have you invited God to show you the deeper source beneath the surface?

Recognize the Mind Is the Battlefield

Before we discuss the process of renewing our minds, we must first establish why it is critical to our freedom. The Enemy's main tactic has always been to attack our minds, which is why the Bible says that the primary way to experience transformation is to renew our minds. Paul said in Romans 12:2, "Do not conform to the pattern of this world, but be transformed by the renewing of your mind."

The mind is where spiritual warfare occurs. The Enemy cannot control your actions, so his next best option is to influence your thinking, knowing that it will impact your life and the decisions you make. Notice that Paul didn't say the key to transformation is for us to try harder or change our behavior. The key is to have our minds renewed!

From the very beginning, the Enemy's tactic has been to attack our minds. Even in the garden of Eden, he planted doubt in the minds of Adam and Eve by saying, "Did God really say . . . ?" (Genesis 3:1). With that one question, he planted doubt and distorted the truth, which led to their disobedience. Think of the mind as our internal steering wheel. It drives our actions, emotions, thoughts, and words. Proverbs 23:7 says, "As he thinks in his heart, so is he" (NKJV).

We see this principle again in Numbers 13. Moses sent twelve spies to spy out the promised land before they took possession of it. When they came back, ten of them reported, "We seemed like grasshoppers in our own eyes, and we looked the same to them" (verse 33). This scripture always makes me laugh because by saying "and we looked the same to them," they assumed they knew how others perceived them, yet they had no proof.

The thoughts that dominated their minds were "We are too weak. The enemy is too strong. We cannot win." Their insecurity and fear led to a generation of people wandering around in the wilderness for forty years. And it began with an idea that contradicted the truth. The truth was that God had already promised them the land and would fight for them, so they had nothing to fear. Had they embraced that truth, their destiny would have been different.

How to Renew Your Mind

So how exactly do we begin to renew our minds? I would like to suggest three steps that have worked for me. With that said, it's critical to note that these steps are not a one-and-done thing but a lifelong process. This is a daily, ongoing journey that sometimes involves progress but also, at times, setbacks. But over time, transformation takes root.

Step 1: Expose the Lies

Before we can embrace God's truth, we must be aware of the lies we've believed for so long. Here are some examples of lies we believe about God:

- God doesn't really love me.
- God is angry with me.
- God can't forgive me after what I've done.
- If I mess up too much, I'll lose my salvation.

Regarding people, we embrace lies such as

- If I let people in, all they will do is hurt me.
- I'll never be able to be happy again after what they did to me.

Common lies relating to addiction are

- I will never be free from this.
- This is just who I am.

- I need this to cope with life.
- God understands. I can't help it.
- As long as I'm not hurting anyone, it's fine.
- One more time won't hurt.

And the list goes on and on.

I've shared a few soul chains I've overcome, and I've also revealed some lies I believed for many years. Regarding relationships, the central lie that I embraced was, "If I don't find the perfect woman, I'll either be miserable or end up getting a divorce like my family members." Or, "Other people may be able to be happy in marriage, but that's not possible for me." Because of the trauma, these lies, and many others, were so deeply entrenched within me that I had no idea they were controlling and dominating my actions and sabotaging all of my relationships. So I went from one relationship to another, trying to find someone who could meet the requirements of this lie. And sadly, I left behind a trail of broken hearts because no woman I met ever reached the perfect standard I was looking for.

As for the soul chain of sexual lust, the primary lie that had me bound was, "Since marriage probably won't happen, the only safe way for me to fulfill my sexual desires is through self-pleasure, and God must be okay with it. Because if He wasn't, He would have sent me my wife by now." Because I believed that lie, I allowed myself to indulge for years, conditioning my conscience to no longer experience conviction. As a result, I sank deeper and deeper into sin, and the soul chain got stronger and stronger.

With the soul chain of perfectionism, it was, "I should always perform above my expectations for myself. If I don't, I have failed." This permeated every area of my life, including golf, pickleball, and even ministry. When I played golf and had a bad round, I felt like a failure because my self-worth was tied to my performance. It resulted in friends not wanting to play with me because I wasn't a fun person to play with. It also resulted in extreme mood swings depending on how I played. Bottom line: I didn't permit myself to fail—ever. Failure was unacceptable.

These are just a few of the lies that I harbored, but let's turn our attention to you. What are some of the lies you've believed that the Enemy has planted deep within you? I encourage you to take some time and identify them by working through the reflection questions at the end of this chapter. Write them down. Expose them. This is the first step toward renewing your mind.

Step 2: Embrace the Truth

Exposing the lies is just the beginning. These lies must be replaced with God's truth. When we do this, the promise is that we will walk in God's perfect will for our lives. Paul said in Romans 12:2 to "let God transform you into a new person by changing the way you think. Then you will learn to know God's will for you, which is good and pleasing and perfect" (NLT). I love that. It's only when we change the way we think that we will learn to know God's will for our lives.

An excellent parable that illustrates both how easy it is to believe a lie and the transformative power of embracing the truth is the well-known parable of the prodigal son.

In the story, the younger son initially believed a lie. The lie was that he'd be happier away from his father's house. As a result of embracing that lie, he wasted his inheritance, lived in misery, and was left broke, broken, and starving. But then we read in Luke 15:17–18, "When he came to his senses, he said . . . 'I will set out and go back to my father and say to him: Father, I have sinned against heaven and against you.'"

He almost believed another lie: that he would no longer be his father's son, only a servant. He could have believed that because of what he had done, his father would never accept him again. He was dealing with shame, a soul chain that many people deal with. But instead, in that moment, he chose not to focus on the lie but to embrace the truth.

The truth was that he was still his father's son, no matter how far he had fallen, and that he could return home.

What was the result? His father restored him completely, gave him a robe of honor, a ring, and sandals. The trajectory of his entire life was changed because he chose to embrace truth rather than a lie. And that truth is one you may need to embrace, my friend. It is a fact that no matter what you've done, how far you've strayed, or how deep your sin is, God still loves you, and embracing that truth will always lead to your restoration.

The truth I had to embrace about my relationship soul chain was that marriage was designed to be highly fulfilling. What happened in my family does not have to be my reality. I can break the soul chain. As I came into contact with couples who had thriving marriages, this truth became more evident to me. I saw examples of marriages I wanted for myself. For the first time in my life, I saw that it was possible to be married *and* happy. I didn't see pain, heartache, and misery. I saw happiness, bliss, and commitment. So the lie I believed for so long was slowly replaced with the truth about what God intended marriage to be.

As for the soul chain of self-pleasure, I had to accept these fundamental truths: Jesus didn't die on the cross for me to be bound to sin. God intended sexual pleasure to be enjoyed between a husband and a wife, not an individual by themself.

The soul chain of perfectionism is one that I am not bound by, but I do battle it almost daily. One key truth I had to embrace was that my worth is not tied to my performance. My mistakes don't define me. Mistakes can be beneficial if I learn from them. Done is better than perfect. People's approval isn't the ultimate goal; God's is.

So as we did when we exposed the lies, write down some truths that you need to embrace about the soul chains you're dealing with right now. What would God have you embrace that will counter the lies the Enemy wants you to believe?

Step 3: Embed the Word

Now that you've written down these liberating truths, it's time to embed God's Word deep within you. The reason this step is so important is that when you are tempted to believe lies, the Holy Spirit will remind you of biblical truth, which will help you combat those lies (John 14:26). Here are a few that I had to embrace.

First, Ecclesiastes 4:9–10: "Two are better than one, because they have a good return for their labor: If either of them falls down, one can help the other up." Another was Genesis 2:18: "It is not good for the man to be alone. I will make a helper suitable for him." While some can thrive as a single person, for me, this scripture was true. It was not good for me to be alone. I needed a helper to fulfill the purpose God had created for me.

For self-pleasure, I had to embrace Matthew 5:28, which says, "But I tell you that anyone who looks at a woman lustfully has already committed adultery with her in his heart." As much as I wanted to justify it, if I was lusting, I was sinning. Another key biblical truth for me was 1 Thessalonians 4:3–5, where Paul said, "It is God's will that you should be sanctified: that you should avoid sexual immorality; that each of you should learn to control your own body in a way that is holy and honorable, not in passionate lust like the pagans, who do not know God." If God commanded me to be sanctified, that meant it was possible to "learn" how to control my own body rather than be controlled by it.

Finally, for perfectionism, a good scripture is Philippians 1:6, which reminds me that "he who began a good work in you will carry it on to completion until the day of Christ Jesus." I have to remind myself (present tense) that God is continuing to do a work in me and that I'll never reach a state of perfection this side of heaven.

Before we move on, take some time to identify key scriptures that God would have you meditate on that tell the truth about who you are and what you're struggling with. Be sure to study them in the proper context. After doing so, commit them to memory and ask the Holy Spirit to remind you of them when you're tempted to believe the lies.

What This Looks Like

Now that we understand the three steps, it's helpful to see how this plays out practically in real life. A woman named Paula shared her testimony online regarding how God set her free from fear. In her testimony, she acknowledged that this chain of fear had gripped her tightly since childhood. She confessed that even at a young age she had terrible nightmares, which caused her to be afraid to sleep in the room by herself. She was afraid to give answers in school in front of others.

She went on to share that she got married at twenty-one and was so thankful that she finally had a husband to sleep next to each night. But eventually her husband got a third-shift job, leaving her home at night all by herself, and the fears and insecurities crept right back in. She was so dominated by fear that many nights she sat in her home holding a gun. She would stay up all night to ensure she was safe from any predators.

> I had been married for about a year and a half when a strange man came to the door one day. . . . Soon his visits turned into a one-time sexual encounter. Immediately my conscience bothered me and I felt dirty. For the first time in my life I had a fear of God and a fear of hell.

I want you to notice a few things. In our chapter on the impact of soul chains, we discussed their interconnectedness. I highlighted that the Enemy doesn't limit his attacks to just one soul chain but many. Paula's soul chain of fear and insecurity led to her having an affair, which led her husband to eventually leave her and their child. It also resulted in her having an unbiblical fear of God. Then God changed her life and set her free.

> A man on TV by the name of Billy Graham, whom I'd never seen or heard before, began telling the story of Jesus Christ coming from heaven. . . . I wanted this Jesus and what He could give me more than anything else in the world, so at the end of the program I talked to Jesus out loud as a little child would. . . . Immediately, the heaviness of sin and grief lifted that I had been carrying for the previous three months! And something else—fear suddenly left that night! I hadn't even asked Jesus to remove it, but He removed it anyway! I didn't need to keep a gun near me or have lights on anymore. I had peace in my mind and peace in my heart for Jesus just as He'd promised.[1]

While I understand that not everyone has had as dramatic a testimony of God setting them free immediately, Paula's story demonstrates the power of God to set us free from the grip of fear, worry, and anxiety.

Conclusion

Winning the war in our minds is a crucial step toward freedom. However, as I mentioned earlier, this is something you must commit to doing regularly. If renewing your mind becomes a lifestyle, you will inevitably experience genuine transformation.

REFLECTION QUESTIONS

1. What is one repeated thought or belief you've been rehearsing that you now recognize as a lie?

2. How has that lie affected your decisions, relationships, or emotional well-being?

3. Which of the categories of limiting beliefs (spiritual, emotional, generational, sexual, relational, and psychological) most applies to your life right now?

4. What truth from Scripture most directly challenges the lie you've identified?

5. How do you typically respond when negative thoughts or lies enter your mind?

6. Have you created any space in your daily routine to consistently "embed" the Word of God into your mind?

CHAPTER 6

SPIRITUAL WEAPONS THAT WORK

Christopher Yuan grew up in a loving home with atheist parents. His father, Leon, had a dental practice. Christopher attended dentistry school in Louisville, Kentucky, and it looked like he would follow in his father's footsteps. Then Leon discovered Christopher's gay pornography, and Christopher admitted that he was gay. His mother, Angela, "gave him an ultimatum, and Christopher gave his goodbye: 'It's not something I can choose,' he said. 'I was born this way.'"[1]

Angela soon became a Christian and prayed diligently for God to change her son's soul: "God, do whatever You have to do in order to save my son." Meanwhile Christopher began selling drugs and was expelled from school. His party lifestyle and drug addiction increased until the day DEA agents showed up at his apartment and charged him with possession of the equivalent of 9.1 tons of marijuana. He was sentenced to six years in prison.

On his third day Christopher walked past a pile of trash. He thought, "This is my life . . . trash." He also saw a Gideon New Testament, and having nothing else to do, he decided to read it. The truths of God's Word began to embed themselves deeply within him, and his transformation began. The prayers his mother had prayed for years were slowly being answered.[2]

But just as his relationship with God was beginning to grow, Christopher was hit with even more devastating news. A blood test showed that he was HIV positive. Yet as he continued to immerse himself in God's Word, his identity shifted. He no longer identified himself by his sexuality and understood that the opposite of homosexuality is holiness. That discovery would become the thesis of his groundbreaking book *Holy Sexuality and the Gospel*, in which he makes the claim that Christians should not identify as homosexual or heterosexual.

Upon leaving prison, he applied to Moody Bible Institute with references from a prison chaplain, a guard, and a fellow prisoner. He went on to earn his master's degree in exegesis from Wheaton College and a doctor of ministry degree from Bethel Seminary. Christopher Yuan now lives a chaste life and leads a global ministry, where he discusses God's truth and grace regarding sexuality and gender.[3]

Christopher's story, particularly viewed through the lens of his mother, Angela, illustrates the powerful weapons we have at our disposal to not only break through our own soul chains but help others experience breakthrough as well.

In the previous chapter, our focus was on helping you renew your mind, which involves replacing satanic lies with God's truth. But we must understand that freedom isn't simply about having new thoughts. It involves much more. This is because soul chains are not just mental or emotional; they are also spiritual. And if it's a spiritual battle, spiritual weapons are required.

We are reminded by the apostle Paul of this truth in 2 Corinthians 10:3–4: "Though we walk in the flesh, we do not war according to the flesh. For the weapons of our warfare are not carnal but mighty in God for pulling down strongholds [soul chains]" (NKJV).

We have weapons at our disposal that the world doesn't have access to, and they are designed to enable us to wage war against any attack of the Enemy, especially those on our minds. Specific struggles and soul chains cannot be overcome by willpower or good intentions alone. This is what separates Christianity from a self-help program like Alcoholics Anonymous.

I would like to suggest four powerful weapons that God has given us to engage in spiritual warfare. These are not weapons available only to the spiritual elite. They are promised to every believer who wants to experience total freedom and live the victorious life that Jesus died to give them. When used consistently and biblically, like Angela Yuan did, they have the supernatural power to demolish soul chains and usher in true life transformation from the inside out.

Let's explore exactly what these weapons are, how they function, and how you can begin implementing them in your daily life on your journey to freedom.

Weapon 1: Prayer

The first spiritual weapon every believer has access to is prayer. Now, you may be thinking, "Brother Allen, tell me something I don't know." Knowing that this weapon is available, learning how to use it, *and* actually using it are three very different things.

So before we discuss how to use prayer as a spiritual weapon, we must first be convinced that it is one. I need to be transparent here and say that this is one of the weapons I've struggled with the most. I love studying the Bible and worshiping to some of my favorite music, but disciplining myself to be engaged in prayer consistently has always been a challenge for me. And I trust I am not alone. The power of prayer lies in the reality that we are inviting heaven's power into our earthly battles. While it may feel like an exercise in futility to speak words into the air with no answer coming back, throughout Scripture, we find countless examples of how prayer was the turning point that led to victory and deliverance for God's people.

The Prayer of a Barren Woman

In 1 Samuel 1 we find Hannah, a broken and barren woman who desperately wanted to have a child, but the Lord had closed her womb. To make matters even worse, her husband apparently got tired of waiting for her to conceive and took another wife, whose name was Peninnah. "Elkanah had two wives, Hannah and Peninnah. Peninnah had children, but Hannah did not" (verse 2 NLT).

In that society, if a woman wasn't able to conceive, the assumption was that God must be punishing her by closing her womb. Can you imagine the spiritual, emotional, relational, mental, and social pressure she was facing?

To make things worse, the other wife taunted her daily because of her barrenness. "So Peninnah would taunt Hannah and make fun of her because the LORD had kept her from having children. Year after year it was the same—Peninnah would taunt Hannah as they went to the Tabernacle. Each time, Hannah would be reduced to tears and would not even eat. . . . Hannah was in deep anguish, crying bitterly as she prayed to the LORD" (verses 6–7, 10 NLT).

The priest Eli was there, and because her lips were moving but there was no sound, he thought she was drunk. But she replied, "Oh no, sir! . . . I haven't been drinking wine or anything stronger. But I am very discouraged, and I was pouring out my heart to the LORD. Don't think I am a wicked woman! For I have been praying out of great anguish and sorrow" (verses 15–16 NLT).

Notice she was "in deep anguish," "crying bitterly," "very discouraged," and experiencing "sorrow." She was broken. She could have accepted these soul chains of depression, anxiety, and bitterness, but instead, she chose to fight back with the spiritual weapon of prayer.

Eli responded, "'Go in peace! May the God of Israel grant the request you have asked of him.' 'Oh, thank you, sir!' she exclaimed. Then she went back and began to eat again, and she was no longer sad" (verses 17–18 NLT).

Now, if you know the story, you may think, "Well, of course she was no longer sad. God answered her prayer and gave her a son." However, notice that her joy returned *before* she even knew she was pregnant with Samuel. It says in the following verses, "The entire family got up early the next morning and went to worship the LORD once more. Then they returned home to Ramah. When Elkanah slept with Hannah, the LORD remembered her plea, and in due time she gave birth to a son. She named him Samuel, for she said, 'I asked the LORD for him'" (verses 19–20 NLT).

She didn't wait to feel better before she prayed. She didn't wait until she was pregnant to pray. She prayed amid her anguish and pain, and the Lord gave her the peace her broken heart had been desperately searching for.

Maybe your story is similar to Hannah's. Maybe you're dealing with anxiety and depression over a dream you once believed was possible, and instead, you're facing disappointment. Maybe it's a dream to have a child or more children. Maybe you're mourning the dream of having a great marriage or a thriving business, and you find yourself experiencing extreme depression and anxiety. Prayer is a powerful weapon to help break through that soul chain.

The Prayer of a Fearful King

In 2 Chronicles 20, King Jehoshaphat was experiencing a tremendous amount of fear. An enemy army was advancing to attack him, and he was overcome with trepidation. Verse 3 says, "Jehoshaphat was terrified by this news and begged the LORD for guidance. He also ordered everyone in Judah to begin fasting" (NLT).

He could have embraced the fear, but instead he responded in prayer. "O LORD, God of our ancestors, you alone are the God who is in heaven. You are ruler of all the kingdoms of the earth. You are powerful and mighty; no one can stand against you!" (verse 6 NLT).

In verse 12, he admitted he felt powerless, saying, "O our God, won't you stop them? We are powerless against this mighty army that is about to attack us. We do not know what to do, but we are looking to you for help" (NLT).

I love that final line: "We do not know what to do, but we are looking to you for help." And through prayer, the Lord responded and helped him overcome his fear. Verse 15 tells us that a prophet of the Lord said, "Listen, all you people of Judah and Jerusalem! Listen, King Jehoshaphat! This is what the LORD says: Do not be afraid! Don't be discouraged by this mighty army, for the battle is not yours, but God's" (NLT). Perhaps you're dealing with a soul chain of fear that you can't seem to break free from. Intense and focused prayer can set you free. I believe it. Do you?

There are numerous other testimonies in the Bible of saints praying when faced with significant challenges, only to find God responding in powerful ways that confirmed He had heard and was deeply concerned with their prayers.

Using Prayer as a Weapon

Now that we've seen how powerful prayer can be, let's get practical about how we can use this weapon in the battle. The first thing I want to encourage you to do is to be honest with God. Psalm 51:6 says, "Behold, You desire *truth* in the inward parts, and in the hidden part You will make me to know wisdom" (NKJV).

God already knows what you're going through, so don't feel you need the perfect words. You just need an honest heart. Get real with God and tell Him exactly how you feel. And while you're getting honest with Him, call the soul chain what it is. Expose it. Name it. Whether it's fear, unforgiveness, lust, insecurity, anxiety, depression, or bitterness, don't be uncomfortable exposing it for what it is.

Next, when you pray, pray the Word of God back to Him specifically as it relates to your particular soul chain. In other words, don't just pray, "God, help me to overcome my fear." Instead, pray, "Lord, Your Word says You have not given me a spirit of fear but of power, love, and a sound mind.[4] I choose to believe that today." By praying God's Word back to

Him, you're not just expressing your personal desire; you're aligning your heart with what God has already said. You're agreeing with God that what He has said is true. You're boldly declaring the promises of God.

So, yes, we should pray for God's help, but let's not stop there. Take it a step further and speak His truth back to Him, not because He needs to hear it, but because you do.

Next, be sure to invoke the presence of the Holy Spirit. Admit to God that you, in and of yourself, are powerless to overcome this soul chain and that you are desperately dependent on the Spirit's power to break free. Ask the Holy Spirit to do what you are not able to do. Ask Him to renew your mind. Ask Him to reveal the soul chain that is keeping you bound. Ask Him to soften your heart toward it. Ask Him to give you the strength to resist the temptation. This is the type of prayer that brings supernatural change in our lives. (In the next chapter we will discuss the Spirit's role in more detail.)

Next, be sure to pray consistently about your soul chain. We often pray and then assume that our responsibility is fulfilled because we've put the ball in God's court. Similar to renewing your mind, prayer is not a one-time event.

Depending on the type and intensity of the soul chain, it is not broken with just one prayer. It is dismantled through continual prayer and surrender. Set aside time daily to pray specifically about your soul chain, using Scripture once again. Remember Jesus's words when He said in Luke 18:1, "One day Jesus told his disciples a story to show that they should always pray and never give up" (NLT).

At this point, you may be thinking, "Well, I've been praying about this and nothing seems to be changing." Remember that this is just the first of four weapons we must use. When they are all combined, the Enemy doesn't stand a chance against you. And neither does your soul chain. My prayer for you and me is that we never underestimate the power of prayer as we seek freedom from whatever has us bound.

Weapon 2: Community

In addition to prayer, community can be a powerful weapon to neutralize the spiritual attacks of the Enemy in our lives. It's one of the most underestimated spiritual weapons, and I believe the Enemy prefers it that way because soul chains thrive in secrecy, silence, and shame. When we choose to isolate ourselves and "manage" our struggles by ourselves, we cut ourselves off from one of God's most excellent tools for healing.

Nick Stumbo was a senior pastor for ten years. His ministry was thriving, and he had a beautiful family. But behind the scenes, Nick struggled with an addiction to pornography. Though he tried to fight it on his own for years, none of his attempts brought lasting victory. Eventually he confessed his sin, not only to his wife, but to his entire congregation. This confession triggered a series of consequences, including personal shame and damage to his marriage and reputation. Rather than shoot their wounded, Nick's church, along with his wife, worked together to get Nick the help he needed to break through.

When I interviewed him, I asked him a simple question: "How did you break free?" He explained that he had tried multiple approaches in the past to achieve victory, but all of them had failed. What made the difference was when he joined a Pure Desire accountability group. For the first time, he truly experienced freedom. He said, "The process helps you recognize the way that your wounds and trauma from early childhood have created false core beliefs, and I really think the Enemy reinforces those false core beliefs about worthlessness, shame, a false identity, a sense that we have to perform really well to be loved."[5]

The primary key for Nick was accountability and community. He said, "The Pure Desire groups and counseling helped me find healing in those deep places. But the other part of it was really that group environment, because a Pure Desire group isn't just people sitting in a room saying, 'Did you struggle this week? Did you relapse this week?

Did you look at porn this week?' It's much deeper into looking at what is the process that I take into relapse."[6]

Finally, he shared, "In a weekly group environment, I learned to be honest about my patterns, where they started, and what I needed to do to redirect them early on. And usually that meant getting in touch with other men in the group that could support me."[7]

From the beginning, God made it very clear that it's not good for man to be alone (Genesis 2:18). This timeless truth underscores our desperate need for connection, encouragement, and accountability. We all have blind spots in our lives. Therefore, I would like to suggest several ways in which a godly community can help us experience freedom.

Truth-Telling

The blessing of community is that people can see things about our lives that we can't always see ourselves. Our community can help reprogram our minds where they've been programmed to believe lies. For instance, you may say, "I'm not worthy to be loved after what I've done. If only people knew the real me and what I've done, they would never love me."

To which a person in the community could reply, "True love is not based on performance. It's based on commitment. People who will truly love you won't be doing so because of what you do. They will love you despite yourself just as God does." Or perhaps you see your struggle as just a bad habit. Someone in the community can speak truth to you and help you see it for what it really is: a soul chain that's destroying your life.

This is what the prophet Nathan did for David in 2 Samuel 12. David was blind to the weight of his sin with Bathsheba until he was confronted with the truth by the prophet Nathan, at which time he confessed his sin and penned one of the most beautiful psalms about repentance, Psalm 51. This was because someone in his inner circle had the courage to tell him the truth.

Our community's job is to tell us the truth. Our job is to receive it humbly so we can experience true transformation. This is the ideal, but sadly, even many Christians who have community aren't benefiting from it the way God intended. Sometimes it's because we surround ourselves with people who are too afraid to challenge us. Or we aren't honest with ourselves and therefore aren't honest with others who may be trying to hold us accountable. Or perhaps we are not in touch with our community or accountability partners as often as we should be. Therefore, for us to truly benefit from our community, we must engage with it openly and honestly.

Accountability

So what does authentic biblical accountability look like? The first sign is that it combines both truth and love. Ephesians 4:15 tells us to "speak the truth in love" (NLT). This isn't just a command; Jesus modeled it Himself. John 1:14 says that Jesus came "full of grace and truth." He never watered down the truth to make people feel better about themselves. Nor did He beat them over the head so much that they felt condemned. He found the perfect balance between the two. It's not about asking, "Hey, how many times did you mess up today?" It's about saying, "Hey, bro, let's bring this thing into the light and deal with it together. God's not through with you. He's got an awesome plan for your life." The question is transformed from, "How did you mess up this week?" to "What do you need to do differently this week in your relationship with God to experience freedom?"

The second sign of authentic accountability is what I'll call *the shared struggle*. Accountability can be uncomfortable when the person sharing feels as though they are revealing their struggles to someone who appears to be perfect. If what someone shares with you isn't something you're struggling with, share something that you *are* struggling with or did at some point in your life.

Finally, godly accountability should include prayer and encouragement. Accountability partners should pray with and for each other and invoke God's presence. They should also include a strong dose of encouragement, as many who are struggling often feel extremely *dis*couraged.

We all need a safe place to be ourselves and confess our sins. James 5:16 commands us to do so, saying, "Confess your sins to one another and pray for one another, that you may be healed" (ESV). Specifically, when it comes to struggling with sin, confession to God and others can help us experience freedom.

Accountability is not only reserved for after we sin, but it can also aid us beforehand by identifying triggers in our lives that may make us vulnerable.

Encouragement

One of the greatest blessings of community is that we feel seen and valued within it. A favorite tactic of the Enemy is trying to convince you that you are alone in your struggle. Community destroys that lie right away. For example, let's say that someone is battling shame. They may believe the lie, "I'm the only one who struggles with this." That lie loses its power the moment someone else in the community says, "Me too." The moment someone battling shame hears others in their community be vulnerable and transparent in their struggles is the moment that lie is destroyed.

Perhaps a woman is struggling with bitterness over past abuse and trauma and begins to share her pain within a trusted community. She now feels free, loved, and accepted because she's met with grace and prayer rather than judgment.

Let's say that you continually enter into toxic dating relationships. In isolation, it's easy to remain in these relationships. However, a healthy, godly, and vibrant community can see aspects of those relationships that are ungodly and unhealthy, and even give you the courage to make the difficult choice to sever them.

When you seek to break free from a soul chain, it may take time. As time passes, you may become weary of the fight (if I'm being honest).

I know I did for years. You'll need your tribe to rally around you and encourage you, letting you know that you can keep going and that God is proud of you. We need encouragement even after we fall back into sin, because that's when the temptation to walk in condemnation is the strongest. Without community, you miss out on that encouragement and are more prone to wander in defeat than in victory. Sometimes a simple text message, prayer, or coffee conversation can make all the difference in the world.

Sometimes that encouragement comes in the form of giving you the proper perspective. It's easy to have the wrong perspective when you're stuck in a soul chain.

- I'll never get past this.
- I'm not making any progress.
- I'll never have a healthy relationship.
- I'll never be able to experience true joy.

A godly community can help you have the proper perspective when your emotions cloud your judgment. Perspective doesn't dismiss your feelings; it just helps to put them in the appropriate context.

Intercession

The Bible says that sometimes we are just too weak to pray for ourselves. Romans 8:26 says, "The Spirit helps us in our weakness. We do not know what we ought to pray for, but the Spirit himself intercedes for us." Just as the Spirit intercedes for us, so can the body of Christ when we are too weak to pray.

In Mark 2, there is a beautiful story of a man who was paralyzed. The very definition of being paralyzed is when you want to move something but can't. You're stuck. That describes how we often feel when we are battling a soul chain. We feel paralyzed. As much as we may want to move, we just can't seem to. Well, neither could this man in a physical sense. Notice a few things about this story. First, his friends *carried* him. Mark 2:2–3 says, "Soon the house where [Jesus] was staying was so packed with visitors that there was no more room, even outside the door. While he was preaching God's word to them, four men arrived carrying a paralyzed man on a mat" (NLT). God can use people to carry us in prayer when we are too weak to carry ourselves. That's why the paralyzed man needed friends to help him.

Second, his friends were *persistent.* They didn't give up easily. Notice that it was so packed that there was no way to get inside the house where Jesus was preaching, as the crowds surrounded it. It would have been like trying to follow Tiger Woods on the golf course in his prime. As much as you might have wanted to get close, the crowds were just too thick. That is how crowded it was. His friends could have said, "Well, we will try another day because there's no way we will see Jesus today." But they didn't. They didn't give up. Verse 4 says, "They couldn't bring him to Jesus because of the crowd, so they dug a hole through the roof above his head. Then they lowered the man on his mat, right down in front of Jesus" (NLT). They were so persistent that they climbed onto the roof, cut a hole in it, and lowered the man into the house where Jesus was preaching.

Finally, his friends *pointed him to Jesus.* In other words, they spoke to Jesus on his behalf. A great community will always point you back to Jesus, knowing He is the ultimate Healer. They will support you in intercessory prayer in times and seasons when you feel too weak to pray yourself.

Using Community as a Weapon

When wrestling with soul chains, community isn't just helpful; it's essential in your walk. God never intended for us to fight in isolation. Through intercession, we experience the power of others fighting for us when we can't pray for ourselves and feel spiritually dry. With accountability, we create safeguards when temptation tries to get the best of us.

Encouragement gives us the confidence and courage to keep moving forward when we want to stop and retreat. Truth-telling provides a mirror for our blind spots that we may not be able to see for ourselves. Take advantage of this powerful spiritual weapon the way God designed it. In a world celebrating independence, a godly community says, "You don't have to do this alone."

The darkest period of my life was from 2004—when I graduated from seminary—to 2014, when I met my wife and started my YouTube channel. On the outside, I had a thriving career as a well-known and accomplished high school math teacher. On the inside, I was angry, bitter, jealous, lonely, and depressed. But the one bright spot during that time was my community. God had blessed me with a solid group of like-minded single Christian friends, and we did everything together. We went to movies, hosted game nights at each other's homes, went bowling, went out to eat, and even attended church together. That community kept me out of trouble on many occasions when I wanted to call an ex-girlfriend and spend time alone with her.

One particular friend, with whom I am still close today, was named Marvin. Marvin was single just like me, but he was even older than I was! To keep each other accountable, we would often gather at Starbucks on Friday nights to play chess. (This is where my love, and might I say addiction, to chess began.) We wouldn't just play chess; we would talk about life, love, and our faith. Well, something unexpected happened in Marvin's life. He met a beautiful young lady online, and within months he was married. Within a few more months, they were pregnant with their first child. And within a few years they had become a family of five. Little did Marvin know that God had given me a front-row seat to his life. God was showing me what was possible for me. Not only did my community provide support, encouragement, and fellowship, but it also gave me the hope I didn't have, yet desperately needed, in that season.

Weapon 3: Fasting

The third weapon at our disposal to break down soul chains is fasting. Fasting is one of the most overlooked, misunderstood, yet powerful weapons that we as believers have access to. It's also probably one of the most difficult to use. Let's briefly discuss what fasting is, why it's misunderstood, how to fast biblically, specifically for spiritual warfare, and how to combine it with prayer.

In short, fasting is the voluntary abstention from food or, in some cases, from other things, such as social media, for a specific time and purpose. It's much more than just depriving ourselves. It's our way of expressing our utter dependence upon God. When we fast, we essentially say, "God, I need You more than I need this." You may choose to fast for various reasons. You may want to fast to experience a spiritual breakthrough. Or you may fast to simply draw closer to God. Other times, you may choose to fast before making a significant decision. You could fast as an act of repentance. Finally, you may fast when interceding on behalf of someone else.

The big question related to this book is, "How do I fast specifically as it relates to soul chains and spiritual warfare?" First, I encourage you not to view this as a one-and-done thing. If so, you may get discouraged when the struggles remain. To experience actual change, we may need to fast regularly, just as we need to renew our minds and pray regularly.

Next, I encourage you to combine fasting with the other weapons discussed in this chapter—prayer, community, and worship. In Mark 9:17–29, there is a story of a father who brought his demon-possessed son to Jesus and His disciples. They tried to cast the evil spirit out of him but were unsuccessful. Jesus then expressed frustration over their lack of faith and drove out the demon Himself. Afterward, the disciples asked Him privately why they could not drive out the demon, to which Jesus replied, "This kind can come out by nothing but prayer and fasting" (verse 29 NKJV).[8]

What Jesus was saying here is that certain "kinds" of demonic oppression or influence (which is precisely what soul chains are) require a deeper level of spiritual power and intensity. They require a deeper level of spiritual preparation and dependence upon God.

Next, when you are fasting for a spiritual breakthrough, expect resistance. The Enemy doesn't want you to experience freedom and will do all that he can to hinder you, just as he sought to do with Jesus. You may suddenly feel weak, extremely hungry, irritable, or strongly tempted. This is a sign that your flesh is losing control over you and the Spirit is taking over.

Finally, when you fast, replace the time you usually eat with intentional and intimate time with God. This is the key to the entire process because without it, this is nothing more than a glorified diet plan. You must replace your physical food with spiritual food. Replace this time with prayer, worship, and Bible study so your spirit can be fed and strengthened.

Before moving on, we need to understand that fasting is not some magic formula that will solve all our problems overnight. It's also not something we do to prove ourselves to God. It's a powerful expression of our dependence on God and our ultimate desire for intimacy with Him. Combining fasting with other spiritual disciplines sharpens our spiritual focus and puts us in a better position to truly hear and respond to God. Whether you're fasting for spiritual breakthrough or one of the reasons above, invite God's supernatural power into your natural situation, and fast and pray in expectation that God will respond in His way and His time for His purposes.

Weapon 4: Worship

Now we've come to one of my favorite weapons of warfare: worship. Although not mentioned specifically in Scripture as a weapon, worship can be a powerful way to neutralize our flesh and experience spiritual victory. Worship is much more than music or singing. It's an entire posture of our being, a lifestyle even. This brief section will discuss what worship is, why we worship, and most importantly, how worship can be used within spiritual warfare.

What Is Worship?

Worship is the posture of our heart that declares God's worth, regardless of the circumstance. The word "worship" is derived from the Old English word *worth-ship*, meaning to give someone the honor or value they are due. Scripture describes worship as both a lifestyle (Romans 12:1) and an intentional, specific moment where we focus on exalting God above everything else.

Worship is not just an emotional response; it's about aligning our hearts with God's. It's when we boldly proclaim the truth about God even in the midst of our pain, bitterness, brokenness, sin, shame, feelings of worthlessness, or spiritual attack. Worship is a choice. It's not something we do only when we feel good. We may have to force ourselves to do it even when we aren't feeling like it.

Worship is when we declare to the world and the devil, "Regardless of what you throw at me, God still deserves to be worshiped."

Earlier, we referenced Jehoshaphat's prayer to the Lord when he was experiencing fear that the enemy armies of the Moabites and the Ammonites were coming against him in battle (2 Chronicles 20:6–12). Now I want to show you how he used all four of these spiritual weapons. In addition to his prayer, notice that he not only fasted but also encouraged others to fast with him. Verse 3 says, "Jehoshaphat was terrified by this news and begged the Lord for guidance. He also ordered everyone in Judah to begin fasting" (NLT).

But that's not all. He also worshiped! Verse 18 says, "Then King Jehoshaphat bowed low with his face to the ground. And all the people of Judah and Jerusalem did the same, worshiping the Lord" (NLT).

You can read the rest of this story for yourself, but essentially, the result was that God fought on their behalf. What's more important than the *result* is their *response*. They responded with prayer, fasting, and worship regardless of how God responded. And I want you to notice that Jehoshaphat didn't do it alone. He fasted, worshiped, and prayed with his community. All four spiritual weapons were used in conjunction with one another.

When David was on the run from his enemies, he wrote down his worship in the form of psalms. In one such instance, after having lost his son as a result of his adulterous relationship with Bathsheba, we read, "Then David got up from the ground, washed himself, put on lotions, and changed his clothes. He went to the Tabernacle and *worshiped* the LORD. After that, he returned to the palace and was served food and ate" (2 Samuel 12:20 NLT).

Do you see a common theme in these responses? They all responded in worship. Even Jesus, before He endured the agony of the cross, worshiped. After the Last Supper and before going to the garden of Gethsemane, where He would prepare to suffer, Matthew 26:30 says, "They sang a hymn and went out to the Mount of Olives" (NLT). Worship is our response to every trial or soul chain we face.

Why Do We Worship?

When we worship, we are not just responding to what God has done; we are declaring who God is, even when we have yet to experience the breakthrough we desire (see Hannah's story earlier in the chapter). We worship because it realigns our hearts, repositions our focus away from the intensity of our soul chains, and girds us with the truth, power, and faithfulness of our God, who is greater than our soul chains. It helps us to rise above our current circumstances and see our situation from heaven's perspective.

Worship has the power to shift the atmosphere. When we are burdened by shame, fear, anxiety, depression, or condemnation, worship reminds us of the truth amid the lies the Enemy wants us to believe. Worship keeps our emotions in check. When we're feeling defeated, anxious, angry, bitter, or strongly tempted, worship can lift us above those feelings and ground us in truth.

We worship because through worship we are reminded of who God is, who we are in Him, and what He can do even if He hasn't done it yet.

How Do We Worship?

Worship is a full-body experience that extends far beyond the words we sing on Sunday morning. It's a spiritual *discipline*, which means we may not feel like doing it, to the extent that the Bible calls it a "sacrifice of praise" (Hebrews 13:15). Here is the type of worship that, over time, will break down the soul chains in our lives that keep us from the life God promised.

We Worship with Our Words

Whether we sing, pray, or simply speak God's truth aloud, our words are powerful. When we worship, we are declaring God's goodness, His sovereignty, His grace, His love, and His power. All these truths help dismantle the embedded lies in our minds that form the soul chains that ultimately influence how we live. Let's say you are struggling with fear. You may want to find worship songs that help you focus on God's protection. You can declare Psalm 27:1, which says, "The Lord is my light and my salvation—whom shall I fear?"

Let's say you're battling shame. You'll want to find worship music that reminds you of God's grace. You can declare Romans 8:1: "There is now no condemnation for those who are in Christ Jesus."

Battling anxiety? You'll want to find worship songs that remind you of God's sovereignty. These are designed to embed God's truth in your spirit so that the lies slowly begin to lose their grip on you.

We Worship with Our Bodies

When you worship, it's okay to engage your body. The Bible describes various postures of worship, ranging from lifting hands (Psalm 134:2) to kneeling (Psalm 95:6) and even dancing (2 Samuel 6:14). All of these are biblical expressions of worship that reflect a heart that is surrendered, humble, and filled with joy. I grew up in a traditional Baptist church where expressive worship was nonexistent. If you said "Amen" during the sermon, people would look over at you as if to say, "Be quiet!" It wasn't until college that I began to understand the freedom available through worship. It may feel awkward at first, but expressing yourself in worship can be one of the most freeing and spiritually beneficial experiences you can have.

We Worship with Our Minds

Because soul chains are formed in our minds, worship becomes an excellent way for us to refocus on truth. Instead of rehearsing past pain or failures, or playing the what-if game and being overwhelmed by anxiety, we saturate our minds with the truth about God and the truth about our identity in Christ. Here's the principle: You cannot worship and focus on an embedded lie at the same time.

We Worship with Others

Worshiping with others within our community is a powerful experience. Sometimes you may feel too weak to sing, but hearing others declare God's truth on your behalf can be just what you need to lift your spirit. If you are prone to isolation, worshiping with others can be a significant first step toward freedom.

We Worship Through Obedience

Because worship is a lifestyle that extends beyond music, we must ensure that our lives are surrendered to God. Romans 12:1 says, "I appeal to you therefore, brothers, by the mercies of God, to present your bodies as a living sacrifice, holy and acceptable to God, which is your spiritual worship" (ESV).

Considering all of the mercies God has extended toward us, our only acceptable response is a life sacrificed and surrendered to Him. If your soul chain is a sinful habit, this is particularly key to dismantling it. The more small acts of obedience you do, the more sin loses its grip and power over you.

Conclusion

I pray that you are encouraged by Christopher Yuan's story and the faith of his mother, Angela. She had to pray for years to see her son break through. You may have to commit to doing the same. She fasted for thirty-nine days. You may consider fasting as well. I also trust that my story of how my community helped me break free from a dark season of depression gave you hope that God can do the same in your own life. God has given us access to weapons that we can tap into, bringing heaven's power into our earthly situations. My friend, I am convinced this is more than just theory. Not only have I witnessed these principles at work in my own life, but I have also seen how God has applied them to the lives of countless others. And I am just crazy enough to take God at His word! "For the weapons of our warfare are not of the flesh but have divine power to destroy strongholds [soul chains]" (2 Corinthians 10:4 ESV).

But even with all these weapons at our disposal, we must embrace one key truth: Our victory isn't a result of following a ritual; it's based on an ongoing relationship with God. In the following chapter, we will explore the vital role of the Holy Spirit, who empowers us to use each of these weapons. Let's discover how we can finally walk in the Spirit to experience the breakthrough God has promised!

REFLECTION QUESTIONS

1. Which of the four weapons we discussed (prayer, community, fasting, worship) is the most underused in your life, and why do you think that is?

2. When have you seen the power of prayer make a difference in your life or someone else's? What did it teach you about God?

3. How might a godly community help you identify a soul chain you can't see alone?

4. What fears, insecurities, or excuses have kept you from seeking consistent accountability in the past?

5. Have you ever fasted to break a soul chain or gain spiritual clarity? What was the result, or what held you back from trying?

6. What lie has worship helped you fight back against in the past, or what lie do you need to start worshiping your way through today?

7. If you fully embraced all four weapons consistently for the next thirty days, what kind of transformation do you think you would see in your life?

CHAPTER 7

WHEN THE SPIRIT LEADS, CHAINS FALL

Jessica Stephens grew up in church. On Sunday mornings, she would often ask her father if she could accompany him to church. As a seven-year-old girl, she thoroughly enjoyed attending church. She liked the music, but when it came time for the sermon, she would often fall asleep in her mother's arms. One day, her father told her to pay closer attention to the sermon. That Sunday, the pastor was talking about how to hear the voice of God, and he said, "When you get a thought that is not your own, it may be the voice of the Lord."

Even as young as age seven, Jessica was obsessed with her body size. She would pinch and suck in her stomach because she was self-conscious about her appearance. After continuing this behavior for some time, one night she heard a voice in her spirit prompting her to stop. This was the first time she believed she heard the voice of God.

Jessica attended a church that focused on cultivating faith and believing in God for the impossible, and she seldom heard about the grace of God. She was taught at an early age to have a strong work ethic, and if she worked hard, she could expect things to work out in her favor. So she applied that same principle to her relationship with God, but without realizing it, she became a slave to legalism. She began reading the Bible in sixth grade, and by the time she had finished Deuteronomy, she was convinced that the way to get right with God was through obeying the law. She recounts a time when she told her parents she would no longer eat foods like pork and fish with scales. She remembers saying, "I loved this because this was a list of dos and don'ts, and I was a doer, so this is something I'm gonna do."

As she progressed through high school, her relationship with the Lord became increasingly based on rules and morals rather than a genuine intimate relationship. She began attending Princeton University, and for the first time in her life, her formula of "work hard and things will work out for you" wasn't working. She struggled to make it through her first year academically. One day she met a young man on campus who invited her to attend a prayer session at 7:30 a.m. She thought, "There is no way I'm going to attend this. That is just too early!" But she was so empty inside that she knew she needed something. So she decided to attend the prayer meeting.

When she arrived, she witnessed something she had never seen before. Students were kneeling on the ground, praying, worshiping, and crying out to God. Something within her was stirred and she began to think, "I don't know what this is or what these students have, but I want it." To her surprise, she began attending the prayer meeting regularly each morning at seven thirty and didn't miss a single day. She vividly remembers the Spirit revealing to her that she had been approaching her relationship with God in a completely wrong way. It wasn't merely about checking off boxes and adhering to an endless list of rules, but it was about having a genuine relationship with God. It was in that moment that the scales fell from her eyes and she experienced true freedom. She no longer saw God as a harsh taskmaster ready to punish her for every mistake but as a loving Savior who welcomed her, flaws and all, with open arms.[1]

Many of us can relate to Jessica's story. We remember a specific time and place when the Spirit opened our eyes to see the truth for the first time. Prayer, community, fasting, and worship are all weapons we need to employ to experience spiritual victory, but the power behind all of those weapons is the Holy Spirit. Without a deep and intimate relationship with the Spirit, the weapons of our warfare remain impotent. Our prayers are more powerful when the Spirit leads us. Our community is more effective when those within it are walking in the Spirit. We certainly cannot fast without being strengthened by the Spirit. Finally, even Jesus said that He is looking for those who will worship Him in Spirit and truth (John 4:24).

Because the Spirit is the essential power by which we experience true freedom, we will dedicate this entire chapter to uncovering what it truly means to walk in the Spirit and how this intimate relationship with Him is the primary key to lasting victory over any soul chain. Whether it's fear, shame, legalism, perfectionism, addiction, bitterness, or a deep emotional wound, be encouraged that the Bible says in 2 Corinthians 3:17, "Wherever the Spirit of the Lord is, there is freedom" (NLT).

Who Is the Holy Spirit?

Before focusing on what the Holy Spirit does, we must understand who He is. The Holy Spirit is not an "it" or a "force" or some divine "vibe" or a super "boost" for Christians. He is God, the third person of the Trinity, who takes up residence within every believer from the moment of conversion (Ephesians 1:13–14). Notice I said He is a person. That means we can grieve Him, quench Him, listen to Him, lie to Him, follow Him, walk with Him, or even ignore Him (Ephesians 4:30, Romans 8:14).

Interestingly, Jesus said something shocking to His disciples the night before His death. He said in John 16:7, "It is for your good that I am going away. Unless I go away, the Advocate will not come to you; but if I go, I will send him to you."

Jesus said that it's actually better for us to have the Holy Spirit living within us than for Him to remain on earth. The Holy Spirit is described as our Advocate (John 14:26), Teacher, Comforter, the one who convicts, and the one who empowers. He has several ministries:

- The Holy Spirit guides us into all truth. (John 16:13)
- The Holy Spirit strengthens us in our inner being. (Ephesians 3:16)
- The Holy Spirit fills us with the power to overcome sin. (Romans 8:13)
- The Holy Spirit affirms our identity as children of God. (Romans 8:15–16)
- The Holy Spirit intercedes for us when we don't know what to pray. (Romans 8:26)

In summary, the Holy Spirit is the ultimate power behind our transformation. And thankfully, He doesn't just identify what needs to change within us but also gives us the wisdom and strength to actually make the change. You cannot get free from your soul chain of shame, anxiety, addiction, or low self-esteem in your own strength. You overcome by walking in the Spirit . . . every day.

There's much more we could write about the person of the Holy Spirit, but that would require me to write a theology book, so let's move on and explore specific and practical ways in which the Holy Spirit empowers us to tear down soul chains and walk in true freedom.

The Holy Spirit plays a crucial role in enabling us to break free from our soul chains. One of the ways He does this is through the internal witness of the Holy Spirit. The Bible says in John 16:13, "When the Spirit of truth comes, he will guide you into all truth. He will not speak on his own but will tell you what he has heard. He will tell you about the future" (NLT).

Because soul chains are based on deeply embedded lies we've

believed, the Holy Spirit's job is to be the inner voice that replaces those lies with the truth. He reminds us of the truth when we are tempted to believe a lie.

For instance, someone struggling with the soul chain of bitterness and unforgiveness may be tempted to remain bitter and unforgiving. But the Holy Spirit may gently remind you of Paul's words in Ephesians 4:32: "Instead, be kind to each other, tenderhearted, forgiving one another, just as God through Christ has forgiven you" (NLT). He will remind you of how much God has forgiven you and how you are indebted to forgive others because of the forgiveness you've personally experienced.

A person wrestling with the soul chain of legalism—the feeling that you must measure up and perform to earn God's love and approval—may hear the Holy Spirit reminding them, "By grace you have been saved through faith. And this is not your own doing; it is the gift of God, not a result of works, so that no one may boast" (Ephesians 2:8–9 ESV).

A person struggling with lust may recall Jesus's words in Matthew 5:27–28, "You have heard that it was said, 'You shall not commit adultery.' But I say to you that everyone who looks at a woman with lustful intent has already committed adultery with her in his heart" (ESV).

A person dealing with shame and unworthiness may have the Holy Spirit encourage them with Paul's words in Romans 8:1: "Now there is no condemnation for those who belong to Christ Jesus" (NLT). Or the truth in Psalm 103:12: "As far as the east is from the west, so far does he remove our transgressions from us" (ESV).

You get the point. However, we must understand one fundamental principle for this to work: The Holy Spirit can only work with what we give Him. He is limited to what we place in our own spirit. In other words, He can only bring back to our remembrance that which we have already deposited in our spirit. Think of it this way: Let's say you want to purchase a car for $20,000, but you only have $3,000 in your bank account. The bank can only withdraw the amount you have already deposited. This is why the chapter on renewing your mind is so critical to this process, because if you aren't studying scriptures specifically related to your set of soul chains, you are limiting the Holy Spirit's power to remind you of what God's truth is when you are tempted to believe the lies that have taken root.

Another role of the Spirit is to reveal the source behind our soul chain(s). Earlier in the book, I encouraged you to look beyond the symptoms and identify the source behind your actions. The Spirit will shed light on these areas, enabling you to fully understand the root of your actions. However, the next step is perhaps the most important one in this entire book: walking in the Spirit. The Spirit can do His job of revealing the source and reminding you of the truth, but you and I must make the daily conscious choice to walk in the Spirit. But what exactly does that look like?

What It Means to Walk in the Spirit

Far too often, we are guilty of making walking in the Spirit sound like some mystical experience. It's actually relatively easy to understand but more difficult to apply. In its simplest sense, walking in the Spirit is a practical, moment-by-moment decision to surrender to the leadership of the Holy Spirit in every area of our lives. It means we allow the Holy Spirit to guide how we think, make decisions, and respond to specific situations (and even our desires) rather than being dominated by our flesh, emotions, and perhaps past wounds. Later in this chapter, I'll give specific examples of what this looks like, practically speaking.

Paul wrote in Galatians 5:16, "So I say, walk by the Spirit, and you will not gratify the desires of the flesh." The word "walk" here implies movement. It implies progress. It implies direction. Following where the Spirit leads us is a continual choice rather than defaulting to old patterns.

So what does this look like?

Choosing Truth Over Emotions

The first thing we must do is to choose truth over our emotions. Your feelings typically take the lead when you've dealt with a soul chain for a very long time. This is because we are accustomed to doing what feels normal and natural to us. However, when the Holy Spirit reminds you of the truth, you must set aside your emotions and choose to believe the truth in that moment. Your feelings are not always accurate. This is why the prophet Jeremiah said, "The human heart is the most deceitful of all things, and desperately wicked. Who really knows how bad it is?" (Jeremiah 17:9 NLT).

What Jeremiah is saying here is that we cannot solely trust our hearts. Our hearts can and often do deceive us. So when someone is dealing with a soul chain of anxiety, their heart may be telling them, "Things are out of control. What if this happens? What if my worst fear comes true? What if we don't have enough money?" While all of these are valid thoughts, what we need to do in that moment is choose to believe what God says rather than be dominated by our emotions. He is still sovereign. He is in control. He cares for us. He will provide for us.

So when these negative thoughts and emotions emerge, you must stop and ask yourself, "Is what I'm feeling really true?" This is why Paul admonished us in Philippians 4:8, "Fix your thoughts on what is *true*, and honorable, and *right*, and *pure*, and lovely, and admirable. Think about things that are *excellent* and worthy of praise" (NLT).

The Spirit's job is not to suppress your emotions but rather to help you interpret them through the lens of truth. Emotions are not your enemy; they're a gift from God. In fact, they can often be the first sign that something deeper is going on in your heart. Joy, sorrow, anger, fear—each of these emotions can lead you to a deeper understanding of what you value, what you fear, and where you may need healing or truth. Jesus expressed deep emotion during His earthly life, and Scripture shows us that emotions can be righteous, powerful, and redemptive when guided by the Spirit. The key is not to be led by your emotions but to let them lead you to the feet of Jesus.

Spirit-Led Decisions Are Not Always Logical Decisions

Another key principle is that walking in the Spirit is often not logical. What the Spirit asks you to do may not make sense to you. That's often how you'll have confidence that it's Him, assuming it aligns with God's Word. For example, let's say that someone hurt you deeply. Your flesh and emotions will convince you, "*They* need to come to *me* and beg for *my* forgiveness because *they* hurt *me*." But the Spirit may say, "I know they hurt you, but *you* need to be the peacemaker in this relationship and take the first step toward reconciliation." That doesn't make any logical sense, but that's the Spirit prompting you to walk with Him and experience victory in that moment.

Let's say toxic relationships have been an ongoing soul chain for you. You are dating someone, and on paper they seem like a good fit, but you just don't have peace of mind about them. The Spirit may be prompting you to walk away from that "good" relationship to keep you from reinforcing the soul chain of toxic relationships.

Walking in the Spirit doesn't mean just defying all human logic; it means we choose obedience over what feels comfortable or right. It means we choose to obey God's voice over public opinion.

Ananias had to make this same decision in Acts 9:10–17. He was a believer living in Damascus at the time, and God spoke to him in a vision, telling him to go to the house of Judas and anoint a man named Saul from Tarsus. Now, if I'm Ananias, I'm thinking, "Umm, God, You do know this man Saul persecuted the church, right? And now You want me to go and actually *meet* the man *and* lay hands on him so he can see? Won't he kill me like he has persecuted others?" Logically speaking, what God asked him to do made no sense.

So Ananias replied to God and essentially said, "God, I've heard people talking about all of the terrible things he has done. And he has the authority of the Jewish leaders to do it too!"

In other words, what God was asking Ananias to do didn't make sense, but he chose to surrender to what the Spirit was leading him to do. Well, hindsight is twenty-twenty, as they say, and considering the significant contributions the apostle Paul made to the Christian faith, I'd say he made the right decision.

From 2008 to 2014, I was serving as a worship leader at a local church in Dallas, and I absolutely loved it! I got to lead worship on Sundays, preach six to eight times a year, and teach Bible study on Wednesday nights to a small yet committed group of forty to fifty people. During that dark period of my life, that was undoubtedly the highlight. However, around 2013, I began to sense that my season at that church was coming to a close. I can't tell you how or why I felt that way, I just did. There was absolutely nothing wrong at the church. I was even getting paid a nice salary for serving there. Leaving the church and quitting would have been a significant financial sacrifice. At first, I kind of ignored the prompting. But the more I stayed, the stronger the unrest became until I finally yielded to what I now know was the voice of the Spirit and mustered up the courage to leave the church.

It was honestly one of the most challenging decisions I've ever made, but it was the right one, because what happened shortly after that confirmed it. About a month after I left the church, I began praying and asking God what my next move would be. After all, I was a Bible teacher, and I needed to be teaching the Bible somewhere. I started looking on YouTube and noticed a few (and I mean only a few) Christians teaching the Bible online. So I figured I could teach the Bible online just like them, but in a different way. I'd stand out by creating extremely short videos that packed in tons of information. And that's precisely what I did. Within a year, I had my first one thousand subscribers. A few years later, one hundred thousand. Then, more recently, we hit one million subscribers on the channel.

While I don't like to get caught up in numbers, to me, every subscriber is a soul. Every view represents a person who's been impacted by the truth of God's Word. So yes, numbers matter. God expanded my reach from forty to fifty committed Christians in a Wednesday night Bible study to millions of Christians worldwide. But none of that would have happened if I had not yielded to what I believed the Spirit was telling me to do in that moment. The point of this story is that, at the time, it didn't make sense. To quit teaching the Bible, leave my church, and give up my salary when I was dependent on every dollar that came in didn't make sense. But God knew where He was leading me, and He knows where He's leading you. So I encourage you to follow the leading of the Spirit even if at times it doesn't make logical sense.

The Spirit vs. the Flesh (the Daily War)

Three forces oppose our walking in the Spirit. They are the world system, the flesh, and the devil himself. The flesh is the only thing that lives within us. Every one of us has been born with a sinful nature that the Bible refers to as our flesh. The Bible clearly reveals that our sinful nature opposes what the Spirit desires to do in our lives. In fact, the Bible describes this as a frustrating, ongoing internal battle. Galatians 5:17 says, "The flesh desires what is contrary to the Spirit, and the Spirit what is contrary to the flesh. They are in conflict with each other."

Even the apostle Paul expressed his frustration with his inability to overcome his sinful nature completely. Romans 7:15 says, "I don't really understand myself, for I want to do what is right, but I don't do it. Instead, I do what I hate" (NLT).

Boy, do we get it, Paul! If you've been saved for any length of time, you understand this internal struggle. You want so badly to do what is right, but the temptation to yield to your sinful desires is just as strong, and at times it gets the best of you. To help you fully understand precisely what this inner war looks like, I've selected five prevalent soul chains to illustrate what it looks like to walk in the flesh versus the Spirit.

Soul Chain 1: Lust

Let's begin by contrasting walking in the flesh with walking in the Spirit as they relate to the soul chain of lust.

Walking in the Flesh

It's late, and you see something online that arouses temptation. Instead of turning away and inviting God into your moment of weakness, you dwell on it. You make excuses for it. You justify it. You rationalize it. You convince yourself that you'll only look for a bit. And then in a moment of weakness, you give in. Then the guilt follows, and another soul chain quickly emerges: the soul chain of condemnation. You hear that familiar voice repeatedly telling you that God is angry with you and tired of forgiving you for the same sin. So you assume, "Since I've already indulged, there's no point in stopping now. I might as well indulge more."

Walking in the Spirit

The same temptation arises, but you sense that the Spirit is prompting you. You hear the scripture that the Spirit brings to your remembrance. You remember the guilt you experienced last time. You know the pleasure will be temporary, but the pain will last. You remember how it impacted your relationships in the past. So you turn off the screen, pray, and ask God to give you supernatural strength to resist. You even contact your accountability partner in your community and ask them to pray for you. You still feel tempted, but you celebrate having achieved the victory, even if only for that moment.

Soul Chain 2: Isolation

As we've mentioned, one of the weapons of our warfare is community. However, the Enemy wants us to retreat into isolation. Here is the contrast between walking in the flesh and walking in the Spirit.

Walking in the Flesh

After you have a setback or yield to a recurring sin in your life, you withdraw. You ignore people's calls and text messages. You stop going to church. You stop opening up to your accountability partner and even lie to her. You allow the soul chain of shame to convince you that no one understands or would even care anyway. You believe the lie that you're better off by yourself and you'll just handle it alone. Finally, you believe the lie that even God is disappointed in you and wants nothing to do with you.

Walking in the Spirit

You feel tempted to do what you've always done: Isolate. But you hear the Spirit prompting you to do what feels completely uncomfortable: Reach out. So you text a friend and ask if they'd like to connect with you in person or over the phone. You meet with them over a cup of coffee and talk through what you're wrestling with. You show up to your small group even though you don't feel like it. You get over your pride and confess to your small group or accountability partner that you're struggling and need support and prayer. You allow that community or friend to pray for you, speak life into you, and encourage you. Later you think, "I didn't feel like doing this, but I'm so glad that I did."

Soul Chain 3: Perfectionism

One soul chain we haven't discussed in some time is the soul chain of perfectionism, which can truly hinder us from walking in God's intended purpose for our lives. Here's what the contrast looks like.

Walking in the Flesh

You're practicing the piano, and you keep making mistakes. You obsess over getting it perfect. Then the voice starts to creep in, saying you're no good. You're a failure. You'll never get this right. You should quit. You should have mastered this by now. Other people would have gotten this quicker by now. You begin to beat yourself up for minor mistakes and completely dismiss the progress you've made. Then you are dominated by thoughts of how others will perceive you since you aren't perfect. Your entire identity becomes dependent on how well you perform. After a few more mistakes, you give up and conclude that it was a waste of time and that you're a complete failure.

Walking in the Spirit

You are practicing the piano, and you make mistakes, but you know you are doing your absolute best to get it right. Instead of quitting, you celebrate that your mistakes result in your getting better because they're forcing you to practice that section of the music repeatedly. You acknowledge the mistakes you've made but focus more on your progress than perfection. You humbly ask for more help to improve your mistakes so you can play the song better next time. You press through the mistakes and practice, eventually mastering the music.

Soul Chain 4: Unforgiveness

Forgiving others certainly requires us to walk in the Spirit because it opposes everything our flesh naturally wants to do. Here's a picture of it.

Walking in the Flesh

Someone hurt you deeply. You play the offense over and over again in your mind, and the more you do, the more bitter you become. You avoid the person. Every time you hear their name mentioned, your blood begins to boil. You start speaking negatively about them at every opportunity, slandering their reputation. You even secretly wish that harm might come their way. You look for ways to get even with them and make them pay for what they've done. You allow them to completely take up real estate in your mind and emotions. You believe the lie that forgiving them would minimize the pain they caused you. Then you make others pay for the pain they caused you because "hurting people hurt people."

Walking in the Spirit

You still feel the pain. You acknowledge that the pain will never leave you. But you begin to think about how many times you've offended God and how many times He has forgiven you. You immediately become convicted because you are quick to ask God to forgive you and to receive His forgiveness, but you withhold it from the one who hurt you. So you understand that forgiveness is a choice that doesn't negate the pain. You trust in the justice of God to avenge the offense committed against you. You even take time to pray for the offender, even when you don't feel like it. Finally, you reach out to them (if possible) and clearly communicate to them how they hurt you, expressing that you've forgiven them. Your focus is on the present and the future, and you spend minimal time dwelling on the past and harboring bitterness. You enter into another relationship, giving that person the benefit of the doubt rather than making them pay for someone else's sins.

Soul Chain 5: Unhealthy, Toxic Relationships

The Enemy uses unhealthy, toxic relationships to keep us stuck and to steal precious time from us that we can never get back. He wants to convince us that we don't deserve better. Here is the contrast between walking in the flesh and walking in the Spirit.

Walking in the Flesh

You see red flags in the relationship, but you are lonely and decide you'd rather be with the wrong person than be alone. You know you should honor God with your body, but you compromise your value of sexual purity because you fear that if you don't give in, the person will leave. People have tried to tell you that this person isn't good for you, but you ignore them and even attack them, saying they just don't want you to be happy. You find yourself constantly making excuses for the person you're dating. You don't have true peace, but you assume this is the best you'll get, and this is the best you deserve. You also convince yourself that you could fix them if you just had a little more time.

Walking in the Spirit

The Holy Spirit reveals serious red flags in the relationship. You reach out to your spiritual community because you're unsure whether these are true red flags. You schedule time with a trusted older couple to get to know you and your partner, and you sit with them and explain your concerns. You set boundaries so that physical intimacy doesn't blur the relationship. You think about how ashamed you'd feel sharing with the next person you date that you were intimate with this person. You accept the fact that the only one who can change this person is God, and you are not God. After your community confirms that you and this person are unequally yoked, you make the difficult decision to sever the relationship, trusting that God would not want you to settle and that He has someone more compatible for you. In the future, you look for relationships that draw you closer to Christ, rather than those that pull you further away.

These are just five examples, but similar situations arise multiple times a day in our lives, and each time, we face the same decision: "Will I yield to my flesh or walk in the Spirit?" The more we choose to walk in the Spirit, the more the soul chain loses its power over us.

Earlier I mentioned that my wife and I were struggling as new parents because we were both working full-time. In 2021 we hit a crossroads, and something had to give. Life was moving so fast, and we weren't as connected as we wanted to be. At times it felt like we were two ships passing in the night. I was trying to grow the ministry, and she was working for a Fortune 500 company. We both loved what we were doing, but the rigor of two stressful careers was pulling us apart. And now, the very same job we prayed so hard for her to get just three years before was driving a wedge between us and our family. So, apart from me, my wife began seeking God and praying. Over time, the Spirit revealed to her that it was time for her to leave her career and devote her full energy to her home. This came as a massive shock to both her and me. She was a high-income earner, and we were using her job to access benefits for our family. For months, she brushed off what the Spirit was leading her to do, until it became clear that she could ignore it no longer.

"Where are we gonna get benefits from?" she wondered. "Will my husband really be able to support us if I leave my job and salary? What will my contribution really be to this family if I'm not working?" These were just a few of the thoughts and questions swirling around in her mind. Eventually she surrendered to the Spirit's prompting (not mine) and left her job. For some time, she grieved the loss of her career. After all, she had attended school for it and had been working full-time since graduating from college. But gradually the Spirit began to show us both that she had made the right decision. Since she left her career, she has been able to shed the mommy guilt by focusing full-time on our children. She's been able to take better care of herself physically, spiritually, and emotionally. And she has been able to not only support our growing ministry but lead her own ministries in ways she was previously unable to do.

And most importantly, our marriage has never been better. All of this was made possible because she yielded to the Spirit in a decision that, at the time, didn't make sense to her. What might walking in the Spirit look like in your life, both daily as well as with bigger decisions?

How Do We Know We Are Walking in the Spirit?

Indeed we can know whether we are walking in the Spirit on a case-by-case basis, but how can we evaluate our progress over time? The key indicator is whether we are increasing in the fruit of the Spirit. Walking in the Spirit over time should result in more fruit of the Spirit. I recognize this is very difficult to assess, but you'll have to be as objective as possible as you take inventory of your life.

The apostle Paul wrote in Galatians 5:22–23, "The fruit of the Spirit is love, joy, peace, forbearance, kindness, goodness, faithfulness, gentleness and self-control. Against such things there is no law." Everything on this list is diametrically opposed to the soul chains we face in our lives. I'm convinced each fruit answers or replaces a lie we've believed or a wound we've lived.

If shame has been a soul chain, are you embracing God's perfect and divine *love* for you and then extending that *love* to others?

If condemnation has been a struggle, as you live a life of obedience by walking in the Spirit, you should experience a greater sense of *joy* because sin robs you of the joy God intended.

If fear and anxiety have been soul chains for you, are you experiencing more of His *peace* as you trust in God's plan rather than your ability to figure everything out?

If unforgiveness and bitterness were soul chains for you, as you yield to the Spirit, these should be overcome by *forebearance*, *gentleness*, *faithfulness*, and *kindness* in your interpersonal relationships.

As the soul chain of addiction begins to lose its grip on you as you walk in the Spirit, you should experience a greater ability to exercise *self-control*. This doesn't mean you're perfect; it just means you are progressing.

This list of fruit is not produced overnight in our lives. Just as fruit grows gradually on a tree, so it does in our lives. It takes time. And we will constantly be evolving in the fruit of the Spirit. But when we stay connected to the Vine, we will continue to bear fruit. Jesus said in John 15:5, "I am the vine; you are the branches. If you remain in me and I in you, you will bear much fruit."

Notice He didn't say you *may* bear fruit; He said you *will,* which means this is a promise you can take to the bank.

As you continue on this road to freedom, don't just ask, "When will I break this soul chain over my life?" Instead, ask, "What fruit is God growing in me?" Because the evidence of your healing and transformation will be measured by the fruit you bear.

Conclusion

Walking in the Spirit is a daily, moment-by-moment choice we must make because the temptation will always be present to revert to walking in the flesh. Whether it's anxiety, addiction, legalism, perfectionism, or another soul chain, it is impossible to experience continued victory without full reliance on the power of the Holy Spirit. So I encourage you to yield to the still, small voice of the Holy Spirit, who takes up residence within you to lead and guide you into all truth.

REFLECTION QUESTIONS

1. In what areas of your life have you tried to break free in your own strength instead of depending on the Holy Spirit?

2. Which lie do you most struggle to believe—and what truth

does the Holy Spirit want to remind you of when that lie resurfaces?

3. What's one recent moment when you followed your emotions instead of the Spirit's prompting? How might you respond differently next time?

4. Can you think of a time when the Spirit led you to do something that didn't feel logical but was for your good?

5. Of the five soul chains described (lust, isolation, perfectionism, unforgiveness, toxic relationships), which one do you relate to the most, and how would walking in the Spirit change your response to it?

6. When you reflect on the fruit of the Spirit in your life (Galatians 5:22–23), where do you see growth, and where is God still shaping you?

7. What daily practice can you begin (or restart) to better stay in step with the Holy Spirit throughout the day?

PART 3

EMBRACING THE PROMISE

CHAPTER 8

THE CHAIN-BREAKING KING

From the age of five, Brittni remembers growing up in a very dysfunctional home. She would often hear things like "I hate you" or "I wish I had never had you" from her parents. She was also physically abused as a child. The verbal and physical abuse created soul chains of unworthiness and low self-worth. She started looking for love in all the wrong places and eventually gave her virginity away at the tender age of sixteen. Reflecting on this, she said, "My heart was crushed when I found out that he had cheated on me with three different women."[1] Shortly after this discovery, her insecurities led her to go to a nightclub. While there, the security guards lined her up to get onstage to take off her clothes and dance in front of the crowd. Because she had very little respect for herself, she obliged. And that is when everything began. She began receiving affirmations from men she had never heard before. They said things like, "We love you! You're so beautiful!" She not only walked out of that club feeling affirmed, but she also made $160. That was the lie the Enemy planted within her: "If you want to be affirmed and make money, this is the way to do it."

During this time, she battled anorexia and became obsessed with her weight. While at school, one of the guys found out that she was on a diet and introduced her to cocaine, convincing her that it would help her lose weight. She became addicted to cocaine and then to heroin. She lost so much weight that she ended up spending almost a year in a mental institution. In college, she continued to dance at strip clubs to make money, until one night, a movie producer came in and told her he made "romance movies" and if she was interested, she should give him a call. She knew he was talking about pornography, but because she was so broken, it sounded appealing. And so she ended up in the porn industry for the next seven years.

But her story doesn't stop there. She was so addicted to heroin that she ended up trying to quit porn so she could get some help. In the process, she went to stay with her grandmother, who took her to church. It was then that she gave her life to the Lord. You would think that everything in her life drastically changed in that moment, but the Enemy is never happy when he loses one of his own. The insecurities from her past remained. She met a man who claimed to be a Christian and even took her to church with him. But he was a wolf in sheep's clothing, and the Enemy used him to drag her back into the porn industry for another three and a half years.

One day, she was on an airplane traveling to film what would be her final adult scene, and she happened to read Revelation 2:20–22, which says, "You tolerate that woman Jezebel, who calls herself a prophet. By her teaching she misleads my servants into sexual immorality. . . . I have given her time to repent of her immorality, but she is unwilling. So I will cast her on a bed of suffering, and I will make those who commit adultery with her suffer intensely, unless they repent of her ways." This scripture deeply convicted Brittni, and she knew she needed to quit the lifestyle once and for all. She repented of her sin that day and never went back to the porn industry.

But the soul chains of shame and insecurity remained. Though now free from the porn industry, Brittni assumed that because she was "damaged goods," no decent Christian man would ever desire her. Then she met a man named Richard who saw past her past and accepted her just as

Jesus did. They eventually got married and started a family. Yet the insecurities returned. "How will I tell my kids about what I've done one day?" she worried. But over time, the Lord continued to do a radical work of healing in Brittni's life. Now she and Richard run a ministry called Love Always Ministries where they not only help people get free from pornography addiction but also help those in the adult entertainment industry get out and come to Christ. Brittni's story demonstrates the power of Jesus being able to heal and set us free from any soul chain, no matter what it might be.

Now that we've uncovered a process for addressing the chains that have held us back, I want to paint a vivid picture of the life that is possible for you when you experience the freedom God intended for you. Here's the principle: Jesus didn't just come to improve our lives. He came to set us free completely.

Freedom in Christ is not simply about breaking free from your struggles; it's about stepping into a completely new identity and purpose. Too often people focus solely on what they need to overcome, but true transformation happens when we shift our focus to who we are becoming in Christ. This is more than behavior modification; it is an invitation to live as sons and daughters of God, fully restored, fully loved, and fully empowered. Through Christ, we are no longer defined by our past but by the victory He has already secured for us (2 Corinthians 5:17).

In this chapter, we will explore how Jesus's ministry focused on freedom, paint a vivid picture of what freedom truly looks like, and compare bondage and liberty so that we can move beyond mere survival into the abundant life Christ offers.

Jesus's Ministry of Freedom

Jesus demonstrated God's heart for freedom throughout His earthly ministry. He didn't just come to teach or perform miracles; He came to set captives free. Luke 4:18–19 says, "The Spirit of the LORD is upon me, for he has anointed me to bring Good News to the poor. He has sent me to proclaim that captives will be released, that the blind will see, that the oppressed will be set free, and that the time of the LORD's favor has come" (NLT).

He regularly set captives free from various types of soul chains. And if He had the power to do it then, He still has the power to do it today.

Jesus Freed People from Mental and Emotional Soul Chains

It was supposed to be a simple evening journey across the Sea of Galilee. Jesus had just spent the entire day teaching a massive crowd of people by the shoreline. The crowd was so large that He had to teach from a boat. As evening approached, He turned to His disciples and said, "Let's cross to the other side of the lake" (Mark 4:35 NLT). They probably didn't think much of it. Several of these disciples were experienced fishermen—including Peter, James, and John—and they knew this body of water like the back of their hand. They had weathered storms before. The sea was their backyard. So they began their journey, and at first, the water was calm and the wind was steady. Jesus, exhausted from the day, found a cushion in the stern of the boat and went to sleep. Then the storm came. The skies began to darken. Thunder rolled and lightning flashed like spears being thrown from heaven. The waves of the sea rose and slammed violently against the sides of the boat. The wind howled like a wild animal.

Water poured into the boat, soaking their clothes, first to their ankles, then to their knees. Keep in mind, this wasn't a modern-day cruise ship. This was a small wooden fishing vessel being tossed to and fro like a child's toy in a bathtub. These experienced fishermen began to panic. And to their shock and dismay, Jesus was still asleep in the boat. They cried out, "Teacher, don't you care that we're going to drown?"

Jesus rose and cried, "Silence! Be still!" (verses 38–39). And with these three words, the winds and waves ceased. But now these men were even more terrified than they had been before.

They may not have lived with a chronic sense of fear, but their story, and subsequent stories in the Gospels, illustrate that they struggled with something many of us struggle with: a lack of trust in God's presence and power. Notice how their fears caused them to distort the character of Jesus. They assumed He didn't care and was disinterested in their plight. But Jesus stepped in and alleviated their fears. Perhaps your fear isn't the wind and waves. Maybe it's fear surrounding your finances, your future, or your family. But the same Jesus who calmed their fears is present right now to release you from your soul chain of fear.

Jesus Freed People from Sexual Soul Chains

It was just like any other day, but little did she know that today, her life would be changed forever. It was just before noon, the hottest time of the day, when she made her way to the well to draw water. She kept her head down, clutching her water jar, hoping not to run into anyone. Women usually went to the well either in the early morning or in the evening when it was cool. But she avoided those times for fear that the women of the town would judge her. You see, she had a reputation in Sychar, but not the kind you wanted to have. She had been with five different men, but each relationship had failed. Whether they left her, passed away, or pushed her to the side, her scars ran deep. And now she was shacking up with a man who wouldn't even marry her. With each failed relationship, she left emptier than before, like a dried-up well. Her water jar wasn't the only thing she was carrying that day. She was carrying soul chains of shame, rejection, broken trust, fear of being known, and perhaps even bitterness toward God.

I can relate. But at that well, there was someone else waiting for water too. To her surprise, she met a Jewish man at the well that day. In those days, Jews didn't associate with Samaritans. Not only that, but men also didn't associate with women in public. Indeed it was forbidden for a rabbi to do so. So she was shocked that the man struck up a conversation with her.

"Please give me a drink," He said (John 4:7 NLT). As the conversation ensued, He slowly began to peel back the layers of soul chains that had held her bound for so long. She was thirsty but didn't realize that living water was what she really needed.

Then Jesus said something that struck her to her core. "Go and get your husband,"

"I don't have a husband," the woman replied.

Jesus said, "You're right! You don't have a husband—for you have had five husbands, and you aren't even married to the man you're living with now. You certainly spoke the truth!" (John 4:16–18 NLT).

She froze in disbelief, thinking, "How could this man know all of this about me?" She tried to change the subject, but then Jesus revealed Himself to her as the Messiah, and her life was changed forever. She dropped her water jar and ran back to the people she had once avoided. She said to them, "Come and see a man who told me everything I ever did! Could he possibly be the Messiah?" (John 4:29 NLT). And just like that, her story became the bridge He would use to reach the people in her town.

This beautiful story illustrates that Jesus isn't only interested in forgiving us and setting us free from sin but also in giving us a mission and purpose. He gave the Samaritan woman a new identity and purpose. She battled the soul chain of rejection because five men had presumably walked away. She battled the soul chain of shame, hiding from the people in her community. She struggled with the soul chain of identity confusion, believing her identity was tied to a man. The soul chain of fear caused her to be afraid of being fully known and fully loved. Jesus broke every chain in her life and can do the same in ours.

Jesus Freed People from Spiritual Soul Chains

The streets were quiet after an eventful day celebrating the Passover in Jerusalem. A Pharisee named Nicodemus traveled the dusty roads, hoping to avoid being seen. He was a trusted spiritual leader and teacher within the Jewish community, as well as a member of the Sanhedrin, Israel's highest court of religious authority. Everyone knew his name because he was highly respected. They looked up to the old sage and brought him their questions about God. On the outside, it appeared as though he had it all together. He prayed devoutly, fasted regularly, and obeyed the law seemingly without flaw. But inside, there was an emptiness he couldn't quite explain. Despite doing everything as perfectly as he could, the peace he was looking for escaped him. The more rules he kept, the more he found he needed to keep. The harder he tried, the more he realized it wasn't enough. He was tired. So that night, he came looking for Jesus. However, he had to keep it a secret, fearing that people would see him conversing with a controversial rabbi from Nazareth.

Upon finding Jesus, he said to Him, "Rabbi . . . we all know that God has sent you to teach us. Your miraculous signs are evidence that God is with you" (John 3:2 NLT). Then, with one sentence, Jesus shattered his entire perception of righteousness. Jesus replied, "I tell you the truth, unless you are born again, you cannot see the Kingdom of God" (verse 3). Shocked and confused, Nicodemus replied, "What do you mean? . . . How can an old man go back into his mother's womb and be born again?" (verse 4).

Jesus went on to explain that He was talking about a spiritual rebirth, not a physical one. Righteousness could never be earned; it must be received. For the first time, Nicodemus realized that salvation was not about keeping rules but about receiving grace. Although he didn't come to faith that night, it was evident that Jesus had planted a seed in his heart. Later, in John 7:51, when Jesus was being mocked in front of the Pharisees, Nicodemus spoke up and said, "Is it legal to convict a man before he is given a hearing?" (NLT). And after Jesus was crucified, Nicodemus showed up again, this time during the day. He brought seventy-five pounds of costly spices to anoint Jesus's body for burial (John 19:39). Nicodemus had found what his legalistic heart was searching for: freedom through faith. His story in John 3 reminds us that legalism is a soul chain that looks holy on the outside but keeps the heart enslaved to a list of rules and regulations, hindering a person from being truly free.

Perhaps you see yourself in Nicodemus. You read your Bible every day, attend church regularly, and try your best to live a holy life. But somewhere along the way, you believed the lie that God's approval of you is based on how well you perform. Just as Jesus broke through Nicodemus's soul chain, He can do the same for you.

We discussed and described soul chains in chapter 2, but let's briefly recap them here. Spiritual soul chains lead to decreased intimacy with God, feeling distant and disconnected from Him and less sure of our salvation because our lives are characterized by self-righteousness and legalism. Mental and emotional soul chains cause us to live in shame, fear, anxiety, anger, perfectionism, rejection, or, sadly, even unforgiveness, ultimately leading to bitterness. Relational soul chains lead to dysfunctional relationships and isolation. Finally, sin soul chains are characterized by addictions and destructive habits that control our lives, leaving us feeling utterly helpless to break free.

And to make things worse, these are just the symptoms. The consequences of this type of life are a loss of peace, stunted spiritual growth, broken and toxic relationships, and ultimately, a hindered ability to walk in our unique calling and purpose.

Does any of this sound like the life Jesus died on the cross for us to lead? Since that doesn't sound like a life either of us wants to experience, let's discover the life Jesus intends for us to live.

Spiritual Freedom

When spiritual soul chains are broken, it means we are no longer striving to earn God's love; instead, we are resting in the assurance that we are entirely accepted through Jesus. We reject the feeling of never being good enough. We no longer question whether God loves us based on our performance. We fully understand and embrace that God's love for us is consistent. He doesn't love us more when we perform well and less when we fall short. His love is constant. It means we understand that it is impossible to disappoint God because when He chose to save us, He knew every mistake, sin, flaw, and failure we would ever commit, yet He still chose to save us.

Living in spiritual freedom means we still experience conviction over our sin, but we don't live in shame and condemnation. We confess and repent (more on this later), and then we move on. It means that we fully accept the forgiveness, grace, and love He freely gives, even though we don't deserve it. Spiritual freedom means we enjoy the presence of God and intimacy with God, free from the shackles of legalism and performance. We obey God, not out of obligation, but out of love for Him and what He has done for us.

Emotional Freedom

Emotional freedom means no longer being controlled by the pain of our past wounds. We acknowledge them. We learn from them. The pain is still there, but we don't live from a place of bitterness, fear, insecurity, or unforgiveness. Our emotions don't control us. Our pain doesn't define us. We are no longer prisoners of resentment, anger, or the need for validation from others. Instead, we are free to extend grace to ourselves and others as we walk in God's truth. Here are several indicators of the emotional freedom God intends for us to walk in.

Forgiveness: The Key to Emotional Freedom

Cindy Clemishire grew up in a loving Christian home. Her family hosted a traveling evangelist named Robert Morris and welcomed him into their home. But on Christmas Day 1982, her world changed forever. The man she and her family once trusted began grooming her. When the abuse began, he would tell her, "You can never tell anyone, or it will ruin everything."[2]

Over the next few years, the abuse continued, completely warping her understanding of love and identity. "He trained me to believe abuse was love and that my body was not sacred," she said.[3] As she matured, the effects of the abuse began to surface. She dropped out of college, endured multiple divorces, and lived under long-standing shame and confusion. In her victim statement, she said regarding former pastor Robert Morris, "While you built a megachurch . . . I dropped out of college, endured divorces, and struggled with self-worth."[4] For decades she silently carried the weight of what had been done to her.

In 2007 she mustered up the courage to share her story but was silenced by those who heard it. She refused to sign a settlement offer contingent upon her signing an NDA. Years later, she said, "Because I refused to sign the NDA at the age of thirty-seven, I am able . . . to be the voice for so many people who don't have the courage to come forward."[5]

In March 2025, former pastor Robert Morris was indicted on several charges of lewd or indecent acts with a minor. In October 2025, he pled guilty. But what stands out with Cindy's story is her ability to forgive:

> Seventy times seven. I think it's because the wound—something triggers something, and we have to forgive again, and that forgiveness is not for him. It is for me. It is not about his life, and if I ever say, "I forgive Robert," that doesn't mean I like him, that doesn't mean I condone what he did, that doesn't mean that I think he should be a free man roaming the earth without any consequences. It has nothing to do with Robert's life, and has everything to do with mine and my relationship with God, and my relationship with my friends and family.[6]

Cindy acknowledged that the pain of what happened to her remained, but for her to experience total freedom, she needed to forgive the man who stole her innocence from her.

At the core of emotional freedom is forgiveness. Instead of replaying offenses and allowing bitterness to take root, we *choose* to release those who have hurt us, not because they deserve it (as Cindy stated) but because we refuse to let their actions hold us in bondage. This is often easier said than done. As Cindy so beautifully stated, forgiveness is not excusing or forgetting. It is choosing to no longer be chained to the pain. Jesus demonstrated this on the cross when He prayed, "Father, forgive them, for they do not know what they are doing" (Luke 23:34). Think about that for a second. If Jesus can find it in His heart to forgive the very people who were nailing Him to a cross, how much more can we choose (because it is a choice) to forgive those who have offended us?

Many people hold on to resentment and grudges, mistakenly believing that will somehow protect them from being hurt again. But in reality, it keeps us stuck in the past. It drains our emotional energy, steals our joy, and hinders us from experiencing true intimacy with others and ultimately with God.

Forgiveness says, "God, I choose to release the weight of unforgiveness from my heart. I will no longer let bitterness, anger, or resentment control me. Just as You have forgiven me, I will extend that same grace to others, not because they deserve it, but because I refuse to stay in bondage. I surrender the pain, the offense, and the desire for revenge into Your hands. I trust that You are my healer, my vindicator, and my peace. I am no longer chained to the past; I am free in Christ."

Peace: The Ability to Rest in God's Sovereignty

Another key aspect of emotional freedom is peace. Peace doesn't mean everything is perfect in life, but rather, it is a deep, unshakable rest in God's sovereignty. This peace allows us to navigate life's challenges without anxiety, fear, or an overwhelming sense of despair. Instead of living on a perpetual emotional roller coaster, our lives are characterized by peace. We remain steadfast, knowing that ultimately God is in control. Doesn't that sound like a much better way to live?

Jesus promised this kind of peace when He said in John 14:27, "Peace I leave with you; my peace I give you. I do not give to you as the world gives. Do not let your hearts be troubled and do not be afraid."

Many people live with constant stress and worry, fearing the unknown or feeling burdened by things they cannot control. We worry about our *family*. We worry about our *finances*. We worry about our *future*. But peace in Christ says, "God, I'm going to release full control into Your hands. I trust Your plans even when life doesn't make sense. I know that You are working things out behind the scenes, even if I can't see it or understand it. I will no longer be a slave to anxiety, fear, and worry. I will walk in the confidence that Your plans are better than mine. I trust in Your sovereignty."

Freedom from Fear and Insecurity

Another marker of emotional freedom is being set free from insecurity and low self-worth. Insecurity and low self-image are some of the most crippling soul chains that keep people from stepping into the fullness of who God created them to be. God doesn't want us to feel inadequate, unseen, or unworthy, constantly comparing ourselves to others or being consumed by the need to please people instead of God. However, the truth is that our worth is not determined by what we achieve, how we look, or how others perceive us. Our identity is anchored in the One who created us and calls us chosen, loved, and set apart.

A healthy self-image is not about arrogance or self-reliance but seeing yourself as *God sees you*. It's the ability to walk confidently, not because of personal perfection, but because of divine purpose. Here's what it looks like:

- **Knowing you are loved.** You don't have to fight for attention or approval. You are already fully known and deeply loved by God. (Romans 8:38–39)
- **Standing in confidence, not comparison.** You celebrate who God made you to be instead of constantly measuring yourself against others. (Galatians 6:4)
- **Walking in purpose.** You live boldly, knowing that you were created intentionally and that your life carries divine significance. (Ephesians 2:10)
- **Rejecting lies and embracing truth.** You replace thoughts of inadequacy with the truth of God's Word, declaring, "I am chosen, I am equipped, I am enough in Christ." (1 Peter 2:9)
- **Living with joy and freedom.** You stop striving to be what others expect and start walking in the joy and peace of who God designed you to be. (Isaiah 26:3)

Emotional Freedom Means Joy

Joy is one of the most significant markers of true emotional freedom. For many years (yes, years) of my life, I don't believe I truly had joy. My emotional state fluctuated; mostly, it was down. It was because I was constantly comparing my life, financial situation, and marital status to those of others. I allowed my entire identity to be mainly centered around my marital status. My goal was marriage, but this wasn't something I could control. And because I always felt I was behind, I was seldom able to enjoy the season of life God had me in. Many people consider joy an emotion that comes and goes depending on circumstances. That's called happiness, which depends primarily on what "happens." But biblical joy is more profound. It is a state of being that comes from the presence of God.

Joy stems from us taking a step back from our pain, looking at the totality of what God has done for us, and deciding to rejoice. Joy is a choice. We must *choose* joy. It's a conscious decision that says, "God, despite my difficulties, I thank You for saving me. I thank You for providing for me. I thank You for developing my character even in my tests and trials. I thank You that I am still alive. I thank You for forgiving me. I thank You that I know who wins in the end. I thank You that You are still in control and I'll spend eternity with You!"

When we are free from emotional burdens, we wake up with hope, knowing that yesterday's struggles do not define us. We don't need everything in life to be perfect for us to be content. Joy doesn't mean we never face hardship, but it means we are not overcome by it. It means we find reasons to be grateful, even in the midst of trials.

Freedom from People-Pleasing and the Need for Approval

Emotional freedom also means breaking free from the need for constant approval from others. Many live their lives trying to please everyone, fearing criticism or rejection. But when we are emotionally free, we no longer live for people's approval; we live for God.

Paul said in Galatians 1:10, "Am I now trying to win the approval of human beings, or of God? Or am I trying to please people? If I were still trying to please people, I would not be a servant of Christ." Emotional freedom means that we stop being controlled by what others think and instead walk boldly in our calling, secure in the love of Christ.

Freedom in Relationships

Many people are emotionally bound in unhealthy, toxic, or codependent relationships. Emotional freedom means we no longer depend on others for our sense of worth. Instead of being controlled by past wounds, jealousy, or a fear of rejection, we engage in healthy, Christ-centered relationships built on mutual love, open communication, and mutual respect. This freedom allows us to set healthy boundaries without guilt. We no longer feel obligated to stay in relationships that are toxic or drain us spiritually. Instead, we learn to surround ourselves with people who uplift, encourage, and challenge us in our walk with Christ.

Walking in Contentment

Emotional freedom also manifests as contentment in every season. Paul said, "I have learned to be content whatever the circumstances" (Philippians 4:11). When free, we are not constantly chasing the next thing to make us happy: success, material possessions, or relationships. Instead, we find complete satisfaction in Christ.

Embracing Emotional Freedom Daily

Emotional freedom is not a one-time event but a daily choice to trust in God rather than our feelings. It means surrendering our hurts, fears, and insecurities to Him, knowing His love is enough to sustain us.

When we walk in emotional freedom, we wake up each day with peace instead of anxiety, joy instead of despair, and faith instead of fear. We no longer carry the weight of past mistakes or other people's opinions. We live with confidence, purpose, and unshakable trust in the God who sets us free.

This is the emotional freedom that Christ offers, a life where we are healed, whole, and fully alive in Him.

Conclusion

What I want you to take away from this chapter is that Jesus's ministry was and is a ministry of freedom. He came to set the captives free. That includes you and me. And if we truly believe that His ministry of freedom extends to this day, then we must also embrace the truth that He desires to set us free as well. If you were discouraged because the earlier chapters vividly depicted bondage, shame, and spiritual defeat, be encouraged to know that freedom is available to you and it's promised. And His power is strong enough to free you to walk into the divine purpose He has for you. Freedom may not happen instantly, and it may not always feel like it's happening, but you can trust that the One who began this work in you will carry it through to completion.

Christ has opened the door to your newfound life of freedom. All that's left is for you to walk step-by-step into the freedom He has promised you.

REFLECTION QUESTIONS

1. Which story of Jesus setting someone free (mentally, emotionally, sexually, or spiritually) resonated most with you? Why?

2. What does emotional or spiritual freedom look like for you personally? How would your life change if you walked in that freedom?

3. Are there areas of your life where you are still striving for God's approval instead of resting in His grace?

4. How has people-pleasing or perfectionism hindered your emotional freedom or ability to walk in your true identity?

5. What lies have you believed about your worth or identity that need to be replaced with God's truth?

6. What steps can you begin taking today to align your thinking, emotions, and relationships with the freedom Jesus died to give you?

CHAPTER 9

WHAT FREEDOM LOOKS LIKE NOW

Caleb had one of the most unique and dysfunctional families. He was raised by not one, not two, but *three* gay parents! His mother and father were both professors, but when he was two years old, they divorced, and both of them went into same-sex relationships. His father had several same-sex relationships, but his mother was in a twenty-two-year monogamous same-sex relationship. His mother and her partner moved to Kansas City, Missouri, while his father stayed in Columbia, also in Missouri. Caleb spent most of his childhood going back and forth between the two homes. His mother and her partner were LGBTQ+ activists and were very invested in the lifestyle. As a result, Caleb was taken to gay bars, gay clubs, campouts, house parties, parades, and just about everything else.

Sadly, the Christians he encountered were hostile toward those in the LGBTQ+ community. In one instance, he recounted seeing Christians throwing water and urine on gay people. In other cases, he saw Christians holding signs saying, "God hates gay people." Not surprisingly, he internalized that Christians were mean-spirited, bigoted, evil people who hated anyone who wasn't straight. This led Caleb to have no desire to be a Christian as he got older. He said, "If this is how Christians are, I can't imagine how awful Jesus was."[1]

But one night during high school, a friend invited him to attend a Bible study. He decided to participate in an effort to expose Christianity, not embrace it. But when he heard the gospel, he discovered that the picture of Jesus he had in his head was drastically different from the Jesus of the Bible. He eventually gave his life to Christ, and his life was changed forever. But this was not without a cost. When he came out to his parents that he was a Christian, they kicked him out of the house. He went on to attend Bible college and seminary, eventually becoming a pastor. Caleb could have assumed that he would be no better than his dysfunctional family. But he began preaching the gospel at various churches in town until one Sunday, he decided to invite his mother. She attended, and then the following Sunday, a couple of elders were waiting for Caleb at the door and said to him, "If you want to keep preaching here, don't you ever bring somebody like your mother again. We don't like those people."[2]

Several years later, Caleb began preaching at a church in Dallas, Texas. He pastored there for three years. His mother's partner had died of cancer, and both she and Caleb's father decided to move to Dallas to be closer to family. Then God did the supernatural. Both of his parents separately asked him if it was okay for them to attend his church. Unlike the previous church, this time his parents were treated with dignity and respect. During the summer of 2013, at the ages of sixty-nine and seventy, his parents both gave their lives to Christ. Caleb continues to preach, write books, and use his testimony to speak across the country, demonstrating that broken backgrounds and complicated relational histories don't disqualify someone from ministry or being used by God. Instead, they can become the context from which a person's greatest ministry emerges.

Caleb's story illustrates the power Jesus has to free us from family dysfunction and redirect our purpose. But even though true freedom is available for us in Christ, it is often misunderstood. As a result, many can be confused about what it really is. That's why, before we can fully walk in the freedom Christ has secured, we must confront the subtle lies that sabotage our ability to receive it. There is a lot of misinformation surrounding the concepts of freedom and deliverance, so we must ensure that the principles of freedom are biblically based and theologically sound.

Now that we have painted a beautiful picture of the freedom Christ promises and provides, let's explore five common myths many Christians have regarding it.

Myth 1: Freedom Means I Will Never Struggle Again

One of the biggest myths about freedom in Christ is that once we "experience it," we will never again struggle with fear, insecurity, anxiety, lustful thoughts, unhealthy relationships, or sinful desires. Some erroneously believe that freedom in Christ means the complete removal of all internal struggles. When they face a battle, they doubt whether they are genuinely free.

Truth 1: Struggle Doesn't Mean Defeat

True freedom is not the absence of struggle but the power to overcome it. The apostle Paul described freedom in this way: "We know that our old self was crucified with him so that the body ruled by sin might be done away with, that we should no longer be slaves to sin" (Romans 6:6). In verse 14, he said, "Sin shall no longer be your master, because you are not under the law, but under grace."

The key here is not whether we struggle but what is ruling us. Elsewhere Paul described the ongoing internal struggle as he contrasted the work of the Spirit within us with our fleshly desires. "The flesh desires what is contrary to the Spirit, and the Spirit what is contrary to the flesh. They are in conflict with each other, so that you are not to do whatever you want" (Galatians 5:17).

Finally, even Paul confessed to his internal struggle in Romans 7:18–19, saying, "I know that good itself does not dwell in me, that is, in my sinful nature. For I have the desire to do what is good, but I cannot carry it out. For I do not do the good I want to do, but the evil I do not want to do—this I keep on doing."

Instead of believing the myth that freedom means never struggling again, embrace the truth that freedom means we now have the power to resist, redirect, and walk in victory. Even when we face battles, we do so from a place of victory, knowing Christ has already broken every soul chain that once held us captive. Walking in freedom means learning how to stand firm, renew our minds daily, and rely on the strength of the Holy Spirit, rather than our willpower. (More on this in the next chapter.)

Along these same lines, we need to understand that we may feel extremely tempted in a particular area, but being strongly tempted does not mean we are not free. Instead of asking, "Why am I still struggling?" ask, "How can I respond to this differently in light of the freedom Christ has given me?" True freedom is not about never facing old battles but having the tools, strength, and faith to overcome them in a way we never could before.

Several years ago, I had the pleasure of interviewing my friend Hope Harris on my YouTube channel. She shared her testimony of how God set her free from self-identifying as a lesbian. At a young age, Hope experienced trauma, which opened the door for a soul chain to take root.

> It started when my mother was murdered in front of my eyes when I was four years old. As I moved through the foster care system, I endured both physical and sexual abuse. It seemed like God had truly abandoned me.
>
> By the time I was in my mid-twenties, I was an out loud and proud lesbian. I publicly advocated for gay rights and same-sex marriage. But

> my world came to a screeching halt in 2006 when I was in a car wreck that almost took my life. Bedridden for a year and a half, I had a lot of time for soul searching. There was a lot of friction in the relationship with my partner because I had been the workhorse of our home, and the accident took that away. I tried meditation, counseling, and other measures to deal with my emotional pain, with varying degrees of success.[3]

Then she experienced the grace of God for the first time in her life, but it wasn't without a cost.

> In 2008, a woman whom I had a crush on invited me on a trip with her to East Texas. I remember her asking me what I most wanted in life, and I told her that I wanted peace of mind and heart. She shared the gospel with me, and I learned that Jesus gives peace that "the world cannot give" (John 14:27). I wanted the peace He had to offer, but I knew it would cost me a lot. On February 14, 2009, I trusted in the free gift of grace available to me through Jesus Christ. I was still in a relationship, and when I told her I had become a Christian, she asked me not to come home again. When I did return, I was shut out of both my house and bank account.[4]

Hope went on to share how her life was transformed, how she joined the church staff, and how she reaches out to self-identified members of the LGBTQ+ community and Christian family members who are impacted by their self-identification. But she also shared this:

> While my feelings and attractions have not changed, what has changed is that, rather than living to please myself, I live to please the Lord. God's Word is the leading force in my life.[5]

The idea that once you are set free, life will be struggle free is a myth. Notice that Hope, along with many others who have come out of the LGBTQ+ community, admitted that she still has attraction for the same sex. The difference now is that she is accessing the power available to her to resist the temptation to act on it. And while she may struggle with these internal desires, her struggle does not mean defeat.

Myth 2: Freedom Happens Instantly and Effortlessly

Many Christians have been deceived into believing that freedom in Christ should happen instantaneously. If they pray, surrender, or attend a deliverance ministry meeting and have someone pray and lay hands on them, they should be instantly "free" in that moment. This can be very discouraging for many because they assume they are not free when they continue to struggle with old patterns.

Truth 2: Freedom Takes Time—and That's Okay

Freedom is a process of transformation, not a one-time event. The Bible doesn't describe freedom as a one-time act or "destination" but rather a journey of transformation.

Philippians 1:6 reminds us that "he who began a good work in you will carry it on to completion until the day of Christ Jesus." This means that total freedom is something God will continue to work in us until we see Jesus face-to-face.

The theological concept of sanctification, which is the process of becoming more like Christ, is not a microwaveable concept. It's more like a Crock-Pot. As 2 Corinthians 3:18 says, "The Lord—who is the Spirit—makes us more and more like him as we are changed into his glorious image" (NLT). Notice the words "more and more." Freedom unfolds over time as truth replaces lies and as obedience reshapes patterns.

If fear is your soul chain, you won't stop being afraid the minute you pray and ask God to take away the soul chain of fear. It means that as you replace fear with faith daily, you will (over time) not be bound by fear. If unforgiveness and bitterness are soul chains in your life, you will, by faith, have to choose to forgive and release this bitterness until it becomes natural for you. If you're struggling with an addiction or a sinful habit, you will experience more freedom the more you rely on the Holy Spirit's power to help you overcome temptation moment by moment.

Myth 3: I'm Not Free Until I Feel Free

The major problem with this is that our feelings are inconsistent and unreliable. Some days, you may feel strong and confident as you walk in freedom. Other days, you may struggle or possibly even be overcome by doubt, fear, anxiety, depression, a sinful habit, or some other temptation, causing you to question whether you are free at all.

If we measure our freedom by our emotions, we will always be tossed around, doubting what God has already done.

Truth 3: Freedom Is Not Always a Feeling

The truth is that freedom in Christ is a fact, not a feeling. We shouldn't dismiss our feelings; they are real. But they aren't always reliable. If Satan can convince you that your feelings are equivalent to truth, then he can keep you bound even when the prison door is wide open. You can be fully forgiven and still *feel* condemned. You can be walking in freedom and still *feel* like a failure. It doesn't mean freedom isn't real; it just means that perhaps your emotions have yet to catch up to God's truth. This is why Jesus said in John 8:32, "You will know the truth, and the truth will set you free."

Notice He didn't say, "You will *feel* free, and that feeling will prove it." He said, "You will know the truth." Freedom starts in the mind, meaning we must believe God's words, even if our emotions say otherwise.

A few verses later, Jesus said, "So if the Son sets you free, you will be free indeed" (John 8:36 ESV). He did not say, "You are free if you feel free." God declares freedom over us, regardless of how we feel at any given moment.

Imagine someone has been locked up in prison for twenty years but was recently released. They may still feel trapped in their old mindset as a prisoner, but their legal status says they are free. Just because they don't feel free doesn't mean they aren't. In the same way, when we are set free in Christ, our spiritual status has changed, even if it takes time for our emotions to catch up.

True freedom says, "I may not feel free in this moment, but I trust that God has set me free, and I will walk accordingly." Instead of asking, "Why don't I feel free?" ask, "What truth do I need to stand on today?" Freedom is not about feeling different; it's about thinking differently and knowing what God has already done.

Myth 4: I'm Forgiven but Not Free to Be Used by God

One of the greatest lies the Enemy can deceive a Christian into believing is that they are too sinful, too broken, or too far gone to be genuinely used by God. He is a master at using shame to cause believers to shrink back and shy away from allowing God to use them.

They may be convinced their past has disqualified them from a life of freedom. They believe that they should live the rest of their lives under God's divine hand of judgment and punishment. Because of a lifelong battle with an addiction, a shameful history of broken, illicit relationships, or a deep sense of shame over past choices, many believe the lie that freedom may be available for others but not for them. This lie is rooted in the false belief that freedom in Christ is something you must earn.

Truth 4: God Can Use Your Past to Fuel Your Purpose

One of the most beautiful sights to see in the body of Christ is when a person allows God to use their past mistakes, failures, and sins as the fuel that ignites their purpose. The Enemy has already gained the victory in your life once, regarding sin and shame. Don't let him win on the back end and keep you from sharing your testimony with the world.

My good friend Joshua Broome was living what many men would call "the dream." He was famous, wealthy, and got to sleep with some of the most beautiful women every day—for a living. As one of the most successful actors in the adult film industry, he had filmed over one thousand explicit scenes. He won significant awards and was even named "Top Male Performer of the Year." On the outside, he had all the material and career success anyone could dream of. But deep inside, he was dying.

Joshua never set out to be in the porn industry. He had legitimate aspirations for becoming an actor. He moved to Los Angeles with a dream of breaking into the Hollywood scene. But after struggling to find work and experiencing rejection after rejection, he was approached by someone in the adult entertainment industry. Lost, discouraged, and deceived, he accepted the "acting gig," a decision that spiraled into a life he never imagined.

At first, the money, attention, and lifestyle were intoxicating. He convinced himself it was just acting. But as time passed, he realized he was losing himself. The more films he completed, the emptier he became. Although surrounded by people, he felt deeply alone. He withdrew from everyone and even isolated himself from his family.

At the height of his "success," Joshua made tens of thousands of dollars a month, yet he could not look at himself in the mirror. He even changed his legal name. At one point, he began to question his existence and even seriously considered taking his own life.

He was bound by the soul chain of shame, convinced that he was too dirty and too far gone ever to be loved by God or anyone else. He was bound by the soul chain of identity distortion, convinced that his worth was tied to his performance, appearance, or approval from others. The soul chain of lust and addiction bound him. The soul chain of isolation gripped him.

That all changed one day when he went to the bank to cash a check. Noticing he looked lost and dejected, the bank teller said, "Joshua, are you okay?" This was the first time in over a year that Joshua heard someone call him by his real name, as he had been using a pseudonym in the industry. That pivotal moment sparked a transformation in him that would change his life.

He left that bank thinking, "Maybe there's more to life than what I'm doing. Maybe there's a way out of this lifestyle." He left the porn industry, reconnected with his mother, and moved back to South Carolina.

Despite being rejected by many employers because of his past, Joshua began working as a fitness trainer and, ironically, met a young lady named Hope. She invited him to church, also ironically named Hope Community Church, where he had a radical encounter with the gospel.

He cried out to Jesus for the first time, and everything changed. He renounced his past, left the industry for good, and started rebuilding his life from the inside out. He and Hope eventually married and now have four sons. Joshua pursued a degree in Christian ministries from Liberty University and now travels worldwide, sharing his story to help others find freedom from shame and discover their identity in Christ. Joshua's story is a beautiful testimony of how God can break the soul chains of shame, lust, addiction, and identity distortion.

If you pay close attention, there is a common theme that runs through all of the stories I've shared in this book. That theme is that we experience the ultimate freedom when we allow God to set us free and use the pain from our past to ignite our purpose.

Joshua Broome and his wife lead a ministry called Finding Hope. Christopher Yuan spreads a message of holy sexuality, helping people find their identity in Christ rather than their sexual orientation. Brittni and her husband, Richard, lead Love Always Ministry. Nick Stumbo leads Pure Desire Ministries, helping men experience freedom from pornography addiction. Cindy Clemishire uses her voice to provide hope and healing to those who have been sexually abused. Caleb Kaltenbach founded The Messy Grace Group, where he helps churches love and foster community with LGBTQ+ individuals without sacrificing theological convictions. Hope Harris ministers to those who currently self-identify as LGBTQ+, providing hope and freedom. Taylor Alesia utilizes her voice on YouTube to help young women understand their worth in Christ and deepen their relationship with Jesus. Walking in your purpose should be a divine by-product of your freedom.

Instead of asking, "Can God really use me despite what I've done?" ask, "How can I use my past experiences to glorify God and walk in my divine purpose?" No matter your past, God's mercy is greater.

Myth 5: I Can Be Only Partially Free

Many believers secretly and silently accept this lie. They think, "Sure, maybe I can be free from shame one day, but I'll always struggle with fear." Or, "God can heal me of my anxiety and depression, but I'll never be free from this addiction."

This myth is often rooted in disappointment. After battling the same patterns year after year, we stop praying for or expecting a total transformation. We settle. We manage. We cope. We say things like, "Well, I guess this is just my thorn in the flesh," without really believing that God wants to and can break it.

Truth 5: God Doesn't Do Half Healing

Freedom is holistic. God wants to restore every part of you. What is holistic healing? It's the kind of freedom that touches every part of who you are, not just your outward behavior or spiritual status. God created you as a whole person, consisting of a spirit, soul (your mind, will, and emotions), and body. And because sin and soul chains affect every part of you, God's healing addresses every part of you too.

God heals your spirit: He reconciles you to Himself, restoring your relationship with God.

God heals your mind: He renews your thoughts and breaks the power of lies and mental soul chains.

God heals your emotions: He heals wounds like fear, rejection, shame, and bitterness.

God heals your body: While not everyone is promised physical healing this side of heaven, Christ did die to empower you to overcome physical addictions or patterns that destroy your health.

God heals your relationships: He restores your capacity for intimacy, trust, and healthy boundaries.

God heals your purpose: He realigns your identity and direction so you can walk in your calling with joy.

I want you to imagine a patient who enters the ER with multiple injuries suffered as a result of a car crash (broken arm, head injury, internal bleeding, etc.). Now imagine if the doctor only reset the arm but completely ignored the other injuries. We would consider that medical malpractice. Healing one area while leaving the others unattended doesn't fully restore the person. If a human physician understands this, how much more does the Great Physician?

God is not content to heal your mind, leaving your heart broken. He doesn't just want to heal your addiction without healing your relationship. He is the Great Physician, and His healing plan includes every part of who you are.

Conclusion

Big congrats to you for making it this far. I believe that God is doing something supernatural within you. My prayer for you is that you embrace whatever struggles you have, let God heal you of them, and then become a powerful, unstoppable force committed to allowing God to use all of your flaws and failures to glorify Him.

REFLECTION QUESTIONS

1. Which of the five myths about freedom have you unknowingly believed, and how has that belief shaped how you view your struggle? (Be honest. Do you expect freedom to be instant? Do you assume you're not free if you're still tempted?)

2. After reading the stories of transformation in this chapter, what do they reveal about God's power to redeem and restore? How do these testimonies shift your perspective on what's possible in your own life?

3. In what ways have you measured your spiritual freedom based on feelings rather than truth? What specific scriptures from this chapter can help you re-center your thinking on God's promises rather than your emotions?

4. Have you ever disqualified yourself from freedom because of your past? What part of your story still carries shame, and how can you surrender that to the grace of God today?

5. What area of your life have you stopped praying about because you believed partial healing was the best you could expect? Take a moment to ask the Lord: "What part of me do You still want to heal completely?"

6. How do you believe God can use the pain from your past to propel you into a life of purpose?

7. What is one step of faith you sense God calling you to take today in response to the truths in this chapter? This could be a confession, a prayer, a phone call, a journal entry, or a bold decision. What will your next step be?

CHAPTER 10

STAY FREE

For over twenty years, my friend Jenn Nizza lived her life in deep spiritual darkness, deceived into thinking that she was helping others. At the tender age of thirteen, her mother was deceived into having a tarot card reading at her home. The psychic began to tell thirteen-year-old Jenn things about her life that she could not have known, because Jenn hadn't told anyone any of it. This instantly intrigued her, and the Enemy used it as the gateway to the occult. She began training to tap into demonic forces and use tarot cards for readings. She became obsessed with getting her own readings. As she grew older, she eventually became a full-time psychic medium, communicating with the dead for her clients. She was convinced that she was using these gifts to help people experience peace after losing a loved one, but she was actually practicing something God strictly prohibited.

Jenn was deeply entrenched in the new age world, surrounded by crystals, chanting, burning sage, and spirit guides. But behind the scenes, her life was full of fear, anxiety, and an emptiness she could not shake. She shares stories of how she would be out in public and see demons around her. At times, she would be driving on the freeway and see demons on the road, nearly causing her to stop her car in the middle of traffic, which would have caused an accident. She was even afraid of living alone because of the intense demonic presence around her.

But God had a different plan for her life. Through a series of painful events, Jenn began to question everything. "Why am I still so afraid?" and "Why do I feel so empty even when I'm 'helping' people?" were the thoughts that dominated her mind.

One day the pain was so great that, in a moment of desperation and conviction, she just cried out the name Jesus . . . and everything changed. Jesus saved her. Transformed her. Redeemed her. Forgave her. But what followed wasn't an instant overnight transformation but a robust process of breaking the soul chains of fear, anxiety, control, and spiritual oppression that had held her bound for decades. She truly repented. She renounced the occult, turned away from the demonic lifestyle, and threw away everything connected to it.

She began to devour the Word of God and joined a solid Bible-based church, and now she has been using her testimony for years to speak out boldly against new age practices. But as she was sharing her story with me, toward the end of our conversation, she said something startling. She said that after her salvation and deliverance, she had to guard her freedom because the Enemy continued to try to attack her and pull her back into her new age practices.[1]

Her story illustrates a fundamental principle. Although freedom is promised and embraced, it must be guarded. Imagine a man who's been locked up in prison for years. After serving his time, the prison gates finally open, and he is free for the first time in years. He feels the warmth of the fresh sun on his face. He takes his first breath of fresh air, of freedom, and walks into a world filled with opportunity before him. But here's the reality: Freedom alone isn't enough to keep him from returning to the same poor lifestyle choices that put him in prison in the first place. Unless he is given the tools to live differently and make better decisions, he will likely fall back into the same habits, mindsets, relationships, and choices that landed him in prison to begin with.

Studies show that within three years of being released from prison, nearly two-thirds of released prisoners are rearrested.[2] This isn't because they want to return to prison, but because they never learned how to live completely free and therefore did not guard their newfound freedom. Without accountability, a renewed mindset, healthy environments, support systems, and the proper tools, their freedom is only temporary.

Soul chains work the same way. Through Jesus, our spiritual prison doors have been opened. He has guaranteed our freedom! He has broken every soul chain and calls us into a life of complete and total freedom. But if we don't learn how to live free, we risk drifting back to the very same patterns and lies that once enslaved us. For this reason, our freedom must be guarded, cultivated, and maintained, or the old deceptive lies will come knocking again.

So this chapter isn't just about getting free (we've covered that already); it's about staying free. In the same way that the former inmate needs a new structure for a new life, we, too, need spiritual systems of support and connection that help us walk in sustained victory.

Why Your Freedom Must Be Guarded

Our freedom in Christ is a gift from God, but it's also a responsibility. When Jesus sets us free, we are invited to walk in that freedom, not once but daily. You will be tempted to return to that place of bondage, so guarding this freedom is not optional; it's essential.

The apostle Paul warned believers in Galatians 5:1, "It is for freedom that Christ has set us free. Stand firm, then, and do not let yourselves be burdened again by a yoke of slavery." Notice that Paul affirmed the fact of being set free. But he immediately told the Galatian church that they must stand firm in that freedom. Then he warned them not to allow themselves to be burdened with a yoke of slavery *again*. This suggests that even Paul acknowledged the need to guard freedom. In other words, we can be spiritually free yet mentally or emotionally vulnerable to old patterns.

We see this vividly in the account of the Israelites after the exodus. God miraculously delivered them from Egyptian bondage by splitting the Red Sea, providing manna from heaven, and leading them by a pillar of cloud by day and fire by night. Yet their minds were still in bondage. They were physically free but had the desire to turn back to the same Egyptian bondage they cried out to God to deliver them from. In Numbers 14:3, they cried out, "Wouldn't it be better for us to return to Egypt?" (NLT).

Even though God had promised them a beautiful land flowing with milk and honey, they allowed their fear of the unknown and the discomfort of the wilderness season to make returning to slavery more appealing than trusting God for a new season.

Let's be very clear: Their freedom wasn't taken from them; they were tempted to forfeit it and return. My friend, that same temptation will be there for you and me daily. Old thought patterns will resurface, old sinful habits will call our name, and emotional wounds that have been healed will be poked again. When these things happen, we are faced with a choice: "Do I stand firm, or do I slowly drift back into what once held me captive?" Guarding your freedom isn't about you living in fear; it's about you living with intention.

In the same way a person who has recovered from a life-threatening illness must continue to make healthy choices to maintain their health, so the believer must continue to make daily decisions to protect their spiritual well-being.

In this chapter, we will explore the mindset, habits, and boundaries that will help you stay free, not just for a season but for a lifetime.

The Subtle Drift Back to Bondage

When we think about forfeiting our freedom, we often envision a sort of dramatic fall—a public failure, an intense relapse back into an addiction, or a significant life crisis. But the reality is, for most believers, the return to bondage doesn't happen in a single moment. It occurs gradually over time, similar to weight gain. You don't put on twenty pounds overnight. Weight is gained through several microdecisions about what you eat over an extended period, resulting in a pound here and a pound there. In other words, it's more like a slow leak than a blowout. A compromise here. A habit neglected there. You slowly retreat from the presence of God, and the next thing you know, you find yourself right back where you started.

For this reason, Jesus warned His followers to remain alert. In Revelation 2:4–5 He rebuked the church in Ephesus, not for some major moral failure, but for forsaking their first love. This is often the starting point that leads to a deeper spiritual drift.

The drift can begin with something as small as

- skipping quiet time because you're "too busy,"
- avoiding community and accountability because it feels inconvenient,
- rationalizing a sinful thought or habit because "it's not that bad," or
- entertaining lies or old mindsets without confronting them.

Before you know it, you're spiritually weak because you haven't fed your spirit, and your flesh begins to regain strength. The soul chains that have been torn down are now being rebuilt brick by brick, fueled by apathy and inattention.

Watch Your Triggers

One of the key strategies for guarding your freedom is to become deeply aware of your triggers. These could include people, places, emotions, or situations that make you most vulnerable to falling back into bondage. It's important to note that the trigger isn't necessarily a sin in itself, but it's often the mechanism through which the door to temptation, discouragement, or deception is opened. Living in our newfound freedom means we must be proactive in recognizing and managing our triggers rather than reactive.

For example, someone who has battled an addiction to pornography may find that scrolling through social media late at night looking at random profiles could trigger a relapse. Or being alone at night with their phone could be a trigger.

A person freed from people-pleasing may feel triggered by comparison if they spend too much time on social media looking at everyone else's highlight reels.

The Bible warns us to be self-aware, as we can be easily triggered. First Peter 5:8 says, "Stay alert! Watch out for your great enemy, the devil. He prowls around like a roaring lion, looking for someone to devour" (NLT).

Do you see that? The Enemy always looks for an open door, hoping to entangle you again. Your ability to recognize your triggers is a key to continuing to walk in freedom. Here are a few practical questions to ask yourself to help you identify your triggers:

- What situations or environments may consistently tempt me to return to old patterns?
- Who are the people I tend to compromise with?
- Who are the people who cause me to feel spiritually drained?
- What time of the day am I most vulnerable to sinful thoughts and behaviors?
- What emotions often precede a relapse (boredom, stress, overwhelm, loneliness, anger, exhaustion, etc.)?
- What false comforts do I run to in order to cope with these emotions?

Once you know your triggers, you can take an offensive rather than a defensive stance. You can set up boundaries, tap into your spiritual accountability community, and most importantly, ask the Holy Spirit for discernment in those moments ahead of time.

Stay Connected to the Source

If I could select one thing that is the ultimate key to staying free, it would be staying connected to the Source. In other words, we must remain connected to the One who helped us escape our spiritual prison. Jesus gave us this principle in John 15:5 when He said, "Yes, I am the vine; you are the branches. Those who remain in me, and I in them, will produce much fruit. For apart from me you can do nothing" (NLT).

The big idea Jesus teaches here is the importance of abiding in Him. It's the idea of being totally dependent on Him for our life, sustenance, and strength. So how do we do this?

Daily Devotional

One of the most critical ways to guard your newfound freedom is through consistent, daily, intentional time with God. In the same way that your physical body needs daily nourishment, your spirit needs daily nourishment from God's Word and His presence. We cannot try to put our freedom on autopilot. It must be intentionally nurtured through an intimate relationship with our heavenly Father.

One of the keys to staying connected with God is to have a regular time of prayer and meditation with Him. I know life is busy, and you've probably heard this before. The question is, You've heard it, but are you doing it? Here are a few tips I've found helpful.

1. Find a Place and Time. Find a place to have unhurried and uninterrupted time with God daily. Find a time that you know works well for you, when you'll be able to give Him your undivided attention.

2. Start Small and Stay Consistent. This doesn't have to be for an hour. It may take some time to get there, but start with ten to fifteen minutes of daily practice. It may look like reading a daily devotional or a proverb or psalm, saying a prayer, listening to your favorite worship songs, or a combination of them all. The key is connection. So get creative and switch it up occasionally so that your time with God doesn't get stale and mundane.

3. Let Your Devotions Be Spirit-Led. Don't feel pressured to do the same thing every day simply because that's what you had planned. The Holy Spirit may have a different plan for your time with God that day. Learn to follow where the Spirit is leading you. He may lead you to read. He may lead you to sit and meditate. He may lead you to write in a journal. He may lead you to pray for someone else.

4. Meditate Throughout the Day. Finally, don't just see your daily devotions as the national anthem—something done at the beginning of a game and then forgotten afterward. Be sure to meditate on what the Lord has shown you throughout the day so that your mind is saturated with the Word of God.

If there is one thing I can identify that has resulted in my sustained freedom, it's my daily devotional time with God. I keep it very simple. I wake up and take a one-hour walk (most days) around my neighborhood. For the first fifteen to twenty minutes, I listen to my Daily Audio Bible app. For the next fifteen to twenty minutes, I listen to some of my favorite worship songs. People in my neighborhood probably think I'm crazy because they can't hear what I'm hearing, but they see me lifting my hands and worshiping God on my walk! Then I spend about ten minutes in prayer. I use the ACTS model but modify it slightly to ACTSI.

The *A* is for adoration. I spend time adoring God and telling Him how much I love Him. The *C* is for confession. I confess any known sin to God. The *T* is for thanksgiving. I take some time to thank God for what He has done. This reminds me to always be grateful to God for what He's done. The *S* is for supplication. This is where I get specific and petition God for what I want Him to do for me, my family, and our ministry. The *I* is for intercession. I spend a few minutes praying for people who have asked me to pray for them. Finally, I spend the last few minutes of my walk in silent meditation. Whew! When I start my days like this, my thought-life struggles, joy, peace, and patience with others are all noticeably different than when I miss my time with Him. I am putting God first and allowing His Word to take root in my spirit. I'm not sure how or why it works—it just does. I cannot tell you how transformative this has been for me personally.

When I read the Gospels, I find it interesting that Jesus modeled this for us. You would think, "Why would Jesus, who is perfect and doesn't even possess a sin nature, have to spend regular time with the Father?" Yet we see Him spending time with God throughout the Gospels. Luke 5:16 says, "Jesus often withdrew to lonely places and prayed." Similarly, Mark 1:35 says, "Very early in the morning, while it was still dark, Jesus got up, left the house and went off to a solitary place, where he prayed." If Jesus prioritized His alone time with the Father, how much more should we?

Reflection and Dependence

One of the most overlooked practices is self-examination. Staying connected with God means we are constantly checking in with our hearts. Ask yourself regularly, "Am I drifting? Have I spent time with God today? Have I been slowly returning to old patterns?" The Holy Spirit often reveals small compromises before they evolve into bigger ones. The key is whether we are listening to Him.

Having consistent check-ins with God expresses our complete dependence on Him and forces us to keep a tight leash on our fleshly desires. David demonstrated his awareness of this truth in some of the most beautiful psalms written by him. He said in Psalm 62:5–7, "Let all that I am wait quietly before God, for my hope is in him. He alone is my rock and my salvation, my fortress where I will not be shaken. My victory and honor come from God alone" (NLT).

When you read this psalm, does it describe the type of heart you have for God? A heart that is desperate and dependent upon Him?

We know David was not perfect, but the fact that God called him a man after His own heart indicates that God is not looking for perfection. He's looking for a heart that yearns to be deeply connected to Him.

Setting Up Guardrails

The next natural step we can take to protect our newfound freedom is to establish guardrails to prevent us from reverting to the same unhealthy mindsets we have been freed from. This involves making intentional decisions to set boundaries to protect ourselves. The Bible says in Proverbs 4:23, "Guard your heart above all else, for it determines the course of your life" (NLT).

A boundary or guardrail is a predecided limit that makes it difficult to venture into unsafe territory. It's not about being legalistic but rather about applying wisdom based on understanding how vulnerable we still are to the struggles of our past. In other words, setting up guardrails is not a sign of weakness; it's a sign of wisdom. Paul admonished the believers in Ephesus, saying, "Be careful how you live. Don't live like fools, but like those who are wise" (Ephesians 5:15 NLT).

Setting up guardrails is also a sign of humility. It's our way of admitting to ourselves and others that we are prone to wander and fall. Paul warned in 1 Corinthians 10:12, "If you think you are standing strong, be careful not to fall" (NLT). It's our way of admitting that while we are free, we are still human. It's acknowledging, "I know where I've been, and I have no desire to go back there."

If your soul chain was sexual temptation, unhealthy, toxic relationships, or codependency, you may have to limit or even end contact with certain people. You may have to delete some numbers or block people from contacting you. I established this guardrail when I was dating to protect myself from people I knew weren't right for me. And when I got married, I deleted all the numbers of the girls I had dated before my wife, so there would be no way for me to contact them. You may have to unfriend or unfollow certain people on social media. While dating, you may need to date outside the home to avoid close, private encounters that could trigger temptation. Jennifer and I did this to the best of our ability when we were dating.

If your soul chain was pornography, comparison, or even laziness, you may have to set up a digital boundary. This may include deleting certain apps from your phone. It may involve installing software on your digital devices that monitors the websites you visit and sets up accountability. Since my ministry is primarily online and connected to social media, I cannot delete the apps from my phone. Still, I do silence the notifications so I'm not distracted by them. I also rarely use social media because I want to protect my eyes and mind from what I'm exposed to. You may need to put your phone in another room at night instead of charging it in your bedroom if having the phone in bed triggers your anxiety or lust.

If worry and anxiety are soul chains, you may have to limit how much news you consume daily, which may trigger emotional unrest. If you have a phone addiction, you may have to use screen time limits to ensure you aren't spending an excessive amount of time on it. You may have to limit the time spent talking to certain "friends" who may have a negative influence on your mind.

The point is that you may need to take radical action to maintain your freedom. I believe this is what Jesus was getting at when He said in Matthew 5:29–30, "If your eye—even your good eye—causes you to lust, gouge it out and throw it away. . . . And if your hand—even your stronger hand—causes you to sin, cut it off and throw it away. It is better for you to lose one part of your body than for your whole body to be thrown into hell" (NLT). He was obviously not advocating for self-mutilation but rather taking drastic and radical measures to protect your soul and spiritual health.

A Vision for Your Future

You and I are most effective for God when we live freely. When we are no longer weighed down, distracted, discouraged, and feeling condemned about being bound, we can finally live the life God intended and fulfill our God-given purpose. Freedom is not the finish line; it's the starting point for a life of fulfillment, joy, and purpose. The goal of breaking through is not just to "stop struggling" or to "survive" another day; it's to open your life up to experience true significance as a child of God. Breaking through is not just about being rescued from your past; it's about being positioned for God to call you forward into your spiritual destiny. It's about redefining who you are. Your sinful habits, your emotional wounds, your trauma, or your addiction no longer define you. You are now defined by the calling, the mission, the vision, and the gift God has placed in your life, which your newfound freedom enables you to step into fully.

The most powerful testimony you can have is not just that *you* broke free, but that you are now using your freedom to help others experience freedom. In Luke 22, Jesus predicted that Peter would deny Him three times. But I love the admonition Jesus gave him in verse 32: "When you have turned back, strengthen your brothers." Essentially He said, "Peter, I know you will fail. But after you fail and you are restored, I call you to restore the faith of others who may need courage to stand on their beliefs, just like you did." And that's precisely what we see Peter doing throughout the book of Acts.

That's a beautiful picture of what God desires for you and me. He wants to enable us to transform our pain into our purpose. Your deepest wounds and greatest struggles can become the platform through which your greatest ministry surfaces. When God sets you free, you will always be more sensitive to others who are still bound in the same ways you once were. Lean into that and allow God to use your story to inspire others.

Walking in your newfound victory means setting a new standard for your family. The generational cycles that may have held you and others in your family bound stop with you. Leave a new legacy for your family that will remain for generations to come.

Conclusion

Let me give you a virtual high five because you've come a long way! You've confronted the demonic lies head-on. You've been willing to face wounds that perhaps had been dormant for years. You've exposed the patterns the Enemy has used to keep you bound, and you've embraced the promise of a life of freedom. You've discovered the powerful weapons God has given us to be victorious, such as renewing your mind, prayer, fasting, community, worship, and embracing the power of walking in the Spirit. You now have a clear vision for what freedom in Christ truly looks like. But I want you to remember that as you take each step forward, you may still hear the Enemy whisper, attempting to get you to embrace lies that once held you bound. Expect it. Anticipate it. Prepare for it. Remember Peter's advice in 1 Peter 5:8–9, "Stay alert! Watch out for your great enemy, the devil. He prowls around like a roaring lion, looking for someone to devour. Stand firm against him, and be strong in your faith. Remember that your family of believers all over the world is going through the same kind of suffering you are" (NLT).

You will be tempted to return to what is familiar and comfortable rather than embrace the unknown life of true freedom. Guard your freedom fiercely. Immerse yourself in a community of people who practice the same rhythms and boundaries you've learned. Stay connected to the true Source of your strength through spiritual disciplines. Remember this principle: The Spirit who set you free is the same One who will keep you free.

If and when you fall, don't hide from God and others in shame.

Embrace the forgiveness, grace, and love your heavenly Father wants to pour out on you. His grace is sufficient for you. His love covers a multitude of sins. Every day, there are new mercies waiting for you.

The chains have been broken. Your prison doors have been busted wide open. Your past does not define you. You are defined by your identity in Christ. Don't question your freedom. Instead, remember the words of our Savior, who said in John 8:36, "If the Son sets you free, you are truly free" (NLT).

So walk boldly. Live joyfully. And never, ever go back.

REFLECTION QUESTIONS

1. What specific areas of your life feel most vulnerable to drifting back into old patterns or mindsets?

2. When you sense yourself beginning to drift, what usually comes first: a change in mindset, a drop in discipline, or a specific trigger?

3. What are your personal triggers—people, places, emotions, or situations—that could reopen doors to past soul chains?

4. What guardrails (boundaries, routines, limits) can you put in place this week to help protect your freedom?

5. How consistent is your daily connection with God, and what changes could you make to deepen that connection?

6. Do you view your story of freedom as a tool to help others? If so, who might God be calling you to encourage or disciple?

ACKNOWLEDGMENTS

There are many people whom I would like to acknowledge in this book. I will recognize my dear mother, who sacrificed so much to provide my sister and me with an excellent quality of life as a single mother working several jobs. I cannot think of a time in my life when she wasn't always by my side, supporting me, whether in a dark season or a season of celebration. I want to acknowledge my dear father, who led me to the Lord at the age of eight. He was my first Bible teacher, and I have so many loving memories of having Bible studies with him growing up. However, the person I need to acknowledge and thank the most is my dear and caring wife. Ever since I met her, my life has gone nothing but up in every way imaginable. Her sacrifice and dedication to our family are unmatched. She sets the example of what it means to express the love of Christ, both as a mother and as a wife. To write this book, I've had to spend countless weekends locked in a hotel while she remained home with our two wonderful children. For her sacrifice, I am forever grateful.

NOTES

Chapter 2: Six Chains That Bind the Soul

1. "Strong's Greek: 3053. logismos," Bible Hub, accessed December 18, 2025, https://biblehub.com/greek/3053.htm.
2. "Forgiveness: Your Health Depends on It," Johns Hopkins Medicine, accessed January 16, 2026, https://www.hopkinsmedicine.org/health/wellness-and-prevention/forgiveness-your-health-depends-on-it.
3. Attributed to Pure Life Ministries, https://purelifeministries.org.

Chapter 5: New Mind, New Me

1. Paula, "How God Healed Me from My Fear and Anxiety," HealingfromGod.com, accessed December 18, 2025, https://healingfromgod.com/how-god-healed-me-from-my-fear-and-anxiety.

Chapter 6: Spiritual Weapons That Work

1. "The Power of a Persevering Mother (Christian Men and Their Godly Moms)," *Challies* (blog), April 14, 2017, https://www.challies.com/christian-men-and-their-godly-moms/the-power-of-a-persevering-mother-christian-men-and-their-godly-moms.
2. Jonathan Sprowl, "Christopher Yuan: Human Sexuality and the Gospel," *Outreach Magazine*, June 9, 2020, https://outreachmagazine.com/interviews/56692-christopher-yuan-human-sexuality-and-the-gospel.html.
3. Sprowl, "Christopher Yuan."
4. 2 Timothy 1:7.
5. Allen Parr, "Pastor Confesses Porn Addiction to His Church and Wife

and Then THIS Happened!," posted on June 17, 2022, by THE BEAT by Allen Parr, YouTube, https://www.youtube.com/watch?v=mnPGmbb_32s.

6. Parr, "Pastor Confesses."
7. Parr, "Pastor Confesses."
8. Many modern translations—such as the ESV, NIV, and NLT—don't include the word "fasting" here because it is not found in the earliest and most reliable manuscripts. However, the King James and New King James include it because they were translated from a different family of manuscripts (the Textus Receptus).

Chapter 7: When the Spirit Leads, Chains Fall

1. "I Worshipped Rules Until JESUS Showed Me THIS . . . ," posted on September 22, 2025, by Delafe Testimonies, YouTube, https://www.youtube.com/watch?v=0_uoFqOcrf4.

Chapter 8: The Chain-Breaking King

1. Brittni De La Mora, "How Jesus Rescued Me from a Life of Porn," Premier Christianity, November 26, 2021, https://www.premierchristianity.com/testimonies/how-jesus-rescued-me-from-a-life-in-porn/5768.article.
2. Penelope Rivera, "Cindy Clemishire Testifies She Declined NDA After Alleged Gateway Church Sexual Abuse," KERA News, October 3, 2024, https://www.keranews.org/texas-news/2024-10-03/robert-morris-cindy-clemishire-child-sexual-abuse-texas-gateway-church.
3. "Robert Morris Victim Cindy Clemishire Speaks Out: 'He Built a Very Twisted Framework,'" Beliefnet News, October 2025, https://www.beliefnet.com/columnists/news/2025/10/robert-morris-victim-cindy-clemishire-speaks-out-he-built-a-very-twisted-framework.
4. Kelly Dearmore, "Cindy Clemishire to Robert Morris: 'I Am Not a Victim. I Am a Survivor,'" *Dallas Observer*, October 3, 2025, https://www.dallasobserver.com/news/read-cindy-clemishires-victim-impact-statement-to-robert-morris-40602165/.
5. Rachel Snyder and Cole Sullivan, "Cindy Clemishire Testifies Before Texas House Committee on Alleged Abuse by Gateway Church Founder Robert Morris," WFAA, March 19, 2025, https://www.wfaa.com/article/news/local/cindy-clemishire-testifies-texas-house-committee-on-alleged

-abuse-gateway-church-founder-robert-morris/287-ee39a0a0-9189-451b-a3d4-203cd5f0da2b.

6. Sylvia St. Cyr, "'I Finally Feel Free': Cindy Clemishire Finds Healing After Facing Her Abuser in Court," *The Roys Report*, October 17, 2025, https://julieroys.com/cindy-clemishire-finds-healing-after-facing-her-abuser-in-court.

Chapter 9: What Freedom Looks Like Now

1. Caleb Kaltenbach, "I Was Raised by THREE Gay Parents . . . and Now I'm a Preacher!," posted on October 22, 2021, by THE BEAT by Allen Parr, YouTube, https://www.youtube.com/watch?v=_E9DCY7jAmM&t=1650s.
2. Kaltenbach, "I Was Raised by THREE Gay Parents."
3. "I Felt Like the Lord Abandoned Me," *Watermark Community Church* (blog), April 8, 2017, https://www.watermark.org/blog/i-felt-like-the-lord-abandoned-me.
4. "I Felt Like the Lord Abandoned Me," *Watermark Community Church.*
5. "I Felt Like the Lord Abandoned Me," *Watermark Community Church.*

Chapter 10: Stay Free

1. "Satanic Secrets EXPOSED by Former PSYCHIC," posted on May 6, 2025, by THE BEAT by Allen Parr,YouTube, https://www.youtube.com/watch?v=1kbNER8__Ic&t=1795s.
2. "Prisoners and Prison Re-Entry," United States Department of Justice, accessed December 18, 2025, https://www.justice.gov/archive/fbci/progmenu_reentry.html.

ABOUT THE AUTHOR

Allen Parr is a national speaker, YouTuber, author, and ordained minister. He is the cofounder (with his wife, Jennifer) of Let's Equip, a nonprofit organization that equips Christians and Christian organizations with courses and curricula to serve their biblical literacy and spiritual growth. Allen holds a master of theology degree from Dallas Theological Seminary and has served at several churches in various positions, including as worship pastor and pastor of Christian education. His popular YouTube channel, The BEAT (Biblical Encouragement And Truth) with Allen Parr, encourages millions of believers to live out their true calling as Christians. Allen, Jennifer, and their two children live in Dallas, Texas.